On Celestial Wings

Col Ed Whitcomb

Air Unive
Maxwell Air Forc

D1402420

November 1995

Library of Congress Cataloging-in-Publication Data

Whitcomb, Edgar D.
On Celestial Wings / Edgar D. Whitcomb.
   p.   cm.
Includes bibliographical references.
   1. United States. Army Air Forces—History—World War, 1939–1945. 2. Flight navigators—United States—Biography. 3. World War, 1939–1945—Campaigns—Pacific Area. 4. World War, 1939–1945—Personal narratives, American. I. Title.
D790.W415   1996
940.54′4973—dc20   95–43048
                                                                   CIP

ISBN 1-58566-003-5

First Printing November 1995
Second Printing June 1998
Third Printing December 1999
Fourth Printing May 2000
Fifth Printing August 2001
Sixth Printing April 2003

Disclaimer

This book is dedicated to

Charlie

Contents

Illustrations

Photographs

Foreword

In November 1940, 44 young military cadets graduated from the first Army Air Corps Navigational Class at Miami University in Coral Gables, Florida. The cadets came from all parts of the United States—from the urban areas of the East Coast, westward to the Appalachian Mountains, to the Midwest and prairie states, to the Rocky Mountains, and the West Coast. These young men came from the inner cities, the farmlands, the mountains, and coastal regions, and they were all volunteers. Most were college-educated and in the prime of life. World War II was raging in Europe and it was becoming increasingly difficult for the United States to remain neutral. A few farsighted men in our small Army Air Corps saw the essential requirement for trained celestial navigators in our military aircraft.

The instructor for this navigational class was a 34-year-old high school dropout by the name of Charles J. Lunn. Charlie Lunn had first learned the art of celestial navigation aboard freighter ships in the Caribbean and later as the navigator aboard Pan American Airline planes flying to Europe and Asia.

This book was written by one of those young navigators, Edgar D. Whitcomb, from Hayden, Indiana. Ed Whitcomb tells about these young comrades-in-arms and draws vivid word portraits of them as we learn of their assignments to Air Corps units. We learn how they survived and how some died in World War II. We learn about Ed's own pre-Pearl Harbor assignment with the 19th Bombardment Group at Clark Field in the Philippines and the unfortunate, and perhaps inexcusable, decision not to deploy our B-17 Flying Fortress bombers immediately after the attack on Pearl Harbor resulting in the loss of 40 percent of those aircraft as they sat parked at Clark Field when the Japanese destroyed that vital military air base on the afternoon of 8 December 1941.

CHARLES J. MOTT, Colonel, USAR, Retired

About the
Author

Ed Whitcomb

Edgar ("Ed") D. Whitcomb enlisted in the Army Air Corps in 1940 and was commissioned a second lieutenant the following year with the rating of aerial navigator. He served two combat tours in the Philippines during WWII. After his active military service, he graduated from the Indiana University School of Law. He practiced law in southern Indiana over a period of 30 years including two years as an assistant United States Attorney. A graduate of the Army Command and General Staff Course and the Air Force Staff Course, he served in the Air Force Reserve for 31 years and retired with the rank of colonel. Whitcomb served the State of Indiana as a senator, secretary of state, and governor.

He is the author of *Escape from Corregidor* which was published in Chicago, New York, London, Moscow, and Manila. The book relates Whitcomb's experiences of evading capture, then later being taken prisoner by the Japanese, escaping by an all-night swim from Corregidor, his recapture, and his ultimate repatriation from China as a civilian under an assumed name.

Upon retirement from the practice of law at the age of 68, Whitcomb took to sailing the open seas. He purchased a 30-foot sailboat in Greece and sailed solo across both the Atlantic and Pacific oceans. When not sailing Whitcomb makes his home in the village of Hayden in rural southern Indiana.

Acknowledgments

I am grateful to the following people who contributed so generously to make this book possible: Gen Eugene L. Eubank, Elaine Bath, Ned Vifquain, Phillip Cease, Charles and Sylvia Lunn, Gen Austin J. Montgomery, Joe H. Sherlin, Dr Ron Johnson, Mary O. Cavett, Ruth King, Carl and Shelley Mydans, Frank Kurtz, Elmer Smith, Laura Showalter, Raymond Teborek, William Scott Warner, Carl R. Wildner, George Markovich, Harold C. McAuliff, John W. Cox, Jr., Harry McCool, Robert A. Trenkle, Theodore J. Boselli, Paul Dawson, Merrill and Bette Gordon, Harry Schreiber, Gen A. P. Clark, Harold Fulghum, W. R. Stewart, Jr., Edward M. Jacquet, Dr James Titus, Emily Adams, and the staff at the AU Press.

Introduction

In August 1940 a group of young men from all parts of the United States converged upon Coral Gables, Florida, to become cadets in a military navigation training program. Raised as children of the Great Depression of the 1920s and 1930s, what they wanted more than anything else in life was to fly airplanes. They had all volunteered for the US Army Air Corps with hopes for becoming pilots, but the Air Corps had other ideas. They would become navigators on the world's finest bomber, the B-17 Flying Fortress.

The cadets did not think of themselves as warriors. None of them had ever seen a Flying Fortress. They were civilians who wanted to fly and joining the Air Corps was a means to that end. The thought of flying where man had never flown before or of bombing cities all around the world was farthest from their minds as they struggled with the intricacies of celestial navigation.

On Celestial Wings tells of the development of the first program to mass produce celestial navigators as America geared up for entry into WWII. It also tells of heartrending tragedies resulting from America's lack of preparedness for war and the fight against overwhelming odds in experiences of members of the US Army Air Corps Navigation School class of 40-A. It tells of their honors and victories and their disappointments and bitter defeats in a war unlike any that will ever occur again.

Navigators of the First Global Air Force

The University of Miami band blared its music through the majestic Biltmore Hotel as 44 khaki-clad cadets marched onto the stage of the big ballroom. It was a historic occasion because we were the first graduating class of professional aerial navigators for the United States' military services. We were to become known as the Class of 40-A. On stage with the 44 of us were representatives of the University of Miami at Coral Gables, Florida, the United States Army Air Corps, and Pan American Airways—the organizations that had put together America's first navigation training program. It was among the first programs of World War II in which business, military, and university personnel combined efforts in the interest of national defense.

The date was 12 November 1940. World War II had been raging in Europe for more than a year, and Adolph Hitler had sent his troops into Poland, Norway, Belgium, Luxembourg, and the Netherlands. Fighting, death, and destruction were far away from US shores. America was enjoying peace with a president named Franklin Delano Roosevelt who had vowed that he would never send an American boy to die on foreign soil. Congress had passed laws enacting the draft, but the men on the platform in Coral Gables were not concerned about that. They were all volunteers who anticipated one thing: to fly!

We came in early August 1940 to what became the fountain-head of navigational knowledge.[1] Few people traveled by commercial airlines in those days. We came by bus, boat, train, and automobile from the crowded streets of New York City, the lonely rangelands of Montana, and the peaceful small towns of the Midwest. Many of my classmates were first and second generation Americans of Serbian, Jewish, Italian, Polish, and English extraction. It was an all-American group including, among others, the family names of Markovich, Berkowitz, Boselli, Vifquain, and Meenagh.

The class members were young men in their early twenties, bright-eyed and eager to succeed in navigation school so they could fly. We had only a vague idea of the complexities of celestial navigation. None of us had ever known an aerial navigator nor could have had any idea of the perils the future held for us. We could not have envisioned that we would be flying courses where no man had ever flown, dropping bombs on civilian cities around the world and seeing our classmates shot out of the sky.

My roommate, Theodore J. Boselli, a former champion bantamweight boxer from Clemson University, would later navigate the first presidential plane. Walter E. Seamon, son of the mayor of West Jefferson, Ohio, would also be assigned to the president's plane. George Markovich, a brilliant graduate of the University of California at Berkeley, would guide a plane called the *Bataan* for the great Gen Douglas MacArthur in his flights around the Southwest Pacific. Russell M. Vifquain, the blonde-headed son of an Iowa college professor, had led Iowa State University to be runner-up in the National Collegiate Athletic Association (NCAA) golf competition. In the years ahead he would be with Gen Curtis LeMay dropping tons of incendiary bombs into the crowded heart of Tokyo, Japan. Jay Horowitz, a happy Jewish boy from Sweetwater, Tennessee, would suffer more agony as a prisoner at the hands of the Japanese than anyone could have imagined. These and many others were my classmates as we entered into the academic phase of celestial navigation.

But it was 1940, and we were in the city of Coral Gables. The US was at peace and our thoughts were not of war. Our home during the 12-week course of training was the stately San Sebastian Hotel at the corner of Le Jeune and University streets. In our first military formations we wore T-shirts, civilian clothes, and a variety of uniforms from previous military organizations. We were a second "Coxey's Army" ready to be molded into military men and more importantly, celestial navigators.* One element of cadet life was missing. There were no upper classes, no lower class, and thus no hazing.

Coxey's Army refers to a group of about 500 unemployed persons who marched from Ohio to Washington, D.C., in the spring of 1894 to petition Congress for work on public works projects. The organizer of the march was Jacob S. Coxey.

Capt Norris B. Harbold, a 1928 product of the United States Military Academy at West Point, was in charge of the detachment. He had a history of efforts to promote celestial navigation training in the Air Corps. We conducted close-order drill formations on the streets near the hotel where there was scant vehicular traffic. Coral Gables on the outskirts of Miami was a sleepy and almost desolate city after the big land development boom and later depression of the 1930s. There were dozens of city blocks where streets, sidewalks, curbs, and fire hydrants supported vacant lots overgrown with weeds.

The cadets marched in ragged military formations across the street to the "Cardboard College"—a group of buildings intended to serve the University of Miami until a new campus was established. The university's grandiose plans for new buildings had stopped dead with the advent of the big depression. But the temporary facilities were adequate for our 240 hours of ground training in navigation and meteorology.

The development of the navigation training program had come about in a very unusual way. Gen Delos Emmons, chief of General Headquarters of the US Army Air Corps, had been aboard a giant Pan American clipper on a fact-finding mission to Europe in 1939. All night the big silver clipper lumbered along on its flight from New York to the island of Horta in the Azores. While other passengers dozed, General Emmons observed the plane's navigator industriously plotting his course by celestial navigation. The general stood on the flight deck in awe of the proficiency of the work. Then as the stars faded away in the light of a new day, the navigator pointed to a dark mound on the distant horizon dead ahead of the aircraft.

"That is the island of Horta," announced Charles J. Lunn, the navigator.

"Amazing!" exclaimed the general.

"It would be more amazing if it were not there," replied Lunn matter of factly.[2]

General Emmons had more than a passing interest in this feat of expertise in celestial navigation. Axis victories in Europe suggested alarming possibilities for US involvement in the European war. The Air Corps urgently needed a lot of well-trained and highly skilled celestial navigators. General Emmons knew that there was no program in the Air Corps to do the job although the Air Corps had tried on several occasions to establish celestial navigation schools. At that time, most military flights were conducted within the continental limits of the United States. Therefore, there was little stimulus for flying officers to do more than make a hobby of celestial navigation. A few officers including Norris B. Harbold, Eugene L. Eubank, Albert F. Hegenberger, Glenn C. Jamison, Lawrence J. Carr, and Curtis E. LeMay had taken particular interest in celestial navigation, but by the spring of 1940, the Army Air Corps had only 80 experienced celestial navigators. It would need thousands to man the new bombers on order for the Air Corps.[3]

"How many people could you teach to do this?" Emmons asked Lunn.

"Just as many as could hear my voice," was Lunn's succinct reply.

The conversation planted an idea in the general's mind. With whatever else he may have learned on his fact-finding mission to Europe, he came back to Washington, D.C., with an idea for training navigators.

Upon his return, he contacted Juan Tripp, president of Pan American Airways and Dr B. F. Ashe, president of the University of Miami. Their meetings culminated in an agreement whereby Pan American would provide navigational training with Charles J. Lunn as the chief navigation instructor. The University of Miami would provide food, housing, and classrooms for instruction at the rate of $12.50 per cadet per week. The cadets were in place, and the program was under way even before the agreement was signed.[4]

Charlie Lunn seemed the most unlikely person to be teaching a university class. His academic credentials were woefully deficient. He had no college degrees whatsoever. He had never attended a college or university. The fact was Charles J. Lunn, chief navigation instructor at the University of Miami in Coral Gables, Florida, in 1940, had failed his sophomore year at Key West High School. He was a high school dropout.

Charlie and his sister had stood at the head of their classes in grammar school and in high school until Charlie's interests turned to girls and basketball. At 16 years of age, he was a

4

good enough athlete to draw $10 a game playing for the Key West Athletic Club team. However, as a result of his extracurricular activities, his academic standing declined to the point that he decided to leave school.

Nineteen years later, he found himself standing before a class of college-trained and educated students from all parts of the United States. Many of them had college degrees in engineering, education, and a variety of other fields. It was Charlie's job to train them in the complicated art of celestial navigation.

When Charlie left high school, his father made it clear to him that he was to get himself reinstated in high school or get a job to support himself. Since he had grown weary of dull classroom life, Charlie set out to find a job.

In 1921 there were few employment opportunities in Key West for a 16-year-old high school dropout. Sponging (gathering sponges from the sea) and fishing were about the only jobs available on the island and such jobs were not attractive to young Lunn. The 7th US Navy Base, where many naval vessels stopped for fuel and water, was one of the chief employers in Key West. Charlie was unable to find a job there because 18 was the minimum age for employment with the government.

Like other boys his age, he was fascinated by the foreign ships that came into Key West Harbor. He had talked to sailors about their voyages to far away ports and learned that it would be possible to get a job as an oiler on an oceangoing ship.

So at the age of 16, Charlie took his first job oiling the engine on a freighter of the P & O Steamship Company plying between Key West, Tampa, and Havana. It did not take the lad very long to grow tired of his work in the steaming hot and smelly bowels of the ship. If there were any romance and adventure in that life, they completely escaped him. After a couple of trips, he applied for a job working on the top deck where he would have more opportunity to learn about sailing.

As a deck hand, Charlie was industrious and inquisitive. He asked questions and he studied books until, at the age of 18, he became third mate on his ship.

From childhood, Charlie had heard stories of shipwrecks all along the Florida Keys. Spanish sea captains with millions of dollars in treasure had lost their ships in those waters as they made their way back toward Spain. He also knew the nineteenth century tales of how some Key West natives had ridden mules in the shallow waters along the reefs at night and had held lanterns high on poles to confuse pilots into navigating vessels onto the coral reefs. Natives would then plunder the wrecks. As a result, many Key West merchants sold a large variety of exotic merchandise from such wrecked ships. Wrecking ships, recovering the cargo and selling it resulted in a thriving business in old Key West.

These stories gave young Lunn a good sense of the value of accurate navigation. He became obsessed with the importance of being able to navigate by the stars as a means of maintaining an accurate course on the sea. He studied the stars, and he studied navigation books until spherical trigonometry became commonplace as he worked to master his favorite subject. His diligence in learning the ways of the sea qualified him to be captain of his own ship at the age of 26.

In the early 1930s, an important part of the P & O Steamship Company's business was hauling trains from Key West to Havana. Cubans loaded the trains with sugar. P & O ships then transported the railroad cars laden with sugar back to Key West. From there they traveled on the railroad across the Florida Keys to US markets.

In Havana, Charlie met two people who changed his life forever. The first was an attractive, green-eyed, blond, English girl who worked as a secretary for the P & O office in Havana. After a year-long romance with the handsome young sea captain, she became Mrs Charles J. Lunn. The other person to change his life was Patrick Nolan, a captain for the Pan American Airways Company.

When Pan American pilots moored their flying boats in the Havana Harbor, they were generally near the P & O steam ships. It was a custom for aircrews to go aboard the ships to visit and enjoy good, well-prepared American food. It was on such visits that Captain Nolan became acquainted with Charlie Lunn and his expertise as a celestial navigator.

"Why don't you come up to Miami and make an application for a job as a navigator with Pan American?" Nolan asked Lunn.

Lunn said that he would have to think about it for a while. He did think about it. In 1935 a disastrous hurricane swept across the Florida Keys destroying the rail line that had previously brought the trains to Key West. The P & O lines moved their operation from Key West to Fort Lauderdale. It was then that Charlie made up his mind to apply for a job as a navigator with the Pan American Airways Company in Miami.

At that time, Pan American was extending its aerial routes to distant cities of the world. Among the first people to navigate Pan American's big flying boats to such distant places were Charles J. Lunn and Fred Noonan. The latter name is indelibly written in aviation history as the navigator who accompanied Amelia Earhart on her ill-fated effort to fly around the world. Although Charles J. Lunn is less well known, he had navigated the big Pan American clippers for five years before his fateful meeting with Gen Delos Emmons.

Classes began on Monday, 12 August 1940, with Charlie Lunn as the chief performer. He stood pleading with his fledgling cadets to understand the complicated procedures that he was explaining. There were no teachers' manuals. He was teaching what he had learned at sea and then modified so he could navigate flying machines. Great minds like Nathaniel Bowditch, John Hamilton Moore, Pytheas of Massalia, and many others had unlocked the secrets to using the stars for navigation. Lunn was the link between them and the thousands of young men who would be flying military missions around the world using celestial navigation.

With his fine six-foot physique, Charlie was a handsome figure in his Pan American Airways uniform. However in the classroom at the university, he often appeared in front of his class clad in a round-neck, short-sleeved, knit shirt that exposed the brawny, tattooed arms of a son of the sea.

"Don't write that down," he would plead. "You've got to get it up here in your head. Your notes and papers won't do you any good when you're out over the ocean some night." Navigating over the ocean at night seemed more like a dream than a reality to the cadets. None of us had ever been "out over the ocean" in a plane at night. Nevertheless, Charlie doggedly transferred his grasp of celestial navigation to his struggling students. Little by little we became skilled at celestial navigation.

We received 50 hours of in-flight navigation training flying from the Pan American seaplane base at Dinner Key.* The base was located on the coast five miles from the university. There Pan American converted five of its twin-engine Sikorsky and Consolidated flying boats into flying classrooms for day and night training missions. There were 10 large tables in each plane with maps of the Caribbean Sea area. Each table contained an altimeter, a compass, and an airspeed indicator. A large hatch open to the sky was used for taking celestial observations.

It was said that the ancient flying boats would take off at 115 miles per hour, cruise at 115 miles per hour, and land at 115 miles per hour. Cadet Harold McAuliff described the noise the clipper made in landing as being like the sound of a truck dumping a load of gravel on a tin roof. Antiquated as they were, the planes provided a real-life environment for practicing celestial navigation.

Before a cadet set foot inside the big clipper training ships, he had to spend many hours atop the San Sebastian Hotel at night. There he got acquainted with the best friends he would ever have—the stars and planets. Cadets learned the names and the relative locations of the 50 brightest stars and the planets. Betelgeuse, Arcturus, and Canopus became as familiar as the names of the streets back in their hometowns.

In the classrooms, there were "dry runs" across the Atlantic Ocean from Miami to Lisbon, Portugal, and from Lisbon to New York. These were routes which Charlie Lunn had flown many times. Charlie provided columns of figures representing the altitudes of given stars in degrees, minutes, and seconds. He also provided columns of figures representing the hour, minute, and seconds of each observation. These were to be added and averaged manually before using the almanac and tables to establish celestial fixes along the course. Neither averaging devices nor computers were in use at the time. Navigation was an exercise in mental gymnastics that seemed to have no ending.

---

*By way of contrast, in the mid-1990s fledgling US Air Force navigators selected for the "bomber track" acquire approximately 150 hours of in-flight navigation training by the time they report to their first operational unit.

Academic training quickly revealed that the plane's airspeed indicator did not really measure how fast the plane was traveling. The compass did not tell the exact direction the plane was traveling, and the altimeter did not mark the actual altitude of the aircraft. As an aircraft moves through the air, navigators have to make corrections for such things as temperature, atmospheric pressure, magnetic variation, deviation, precession, and refraction. These were things that Charlie Lunn had learned for himself when he left marine navigation and took to the air.

Days and nights of work and study filled the cadets' lives. As busy as they were the cadets found time for recreation at the beautiful Venetian Swimming Pool and the then uncrowded and uncluttered Miami beach. There were University of Miami football games at the Orange Bowl and dances under the stars at the Coral Gables Country Club. In addition there were many attractive coeds on the campus to keep company with the cadets in their various activities.

Then after 12 short weeks of Charlie Lunn's intensified navigation training, there came the November graduation exercises held at the stately Biltmore Hotel in Coral Gables. Forty-four cadets sat on the stage at the graduation exercises. We listened to speeches by Dr Ashe, Pan American Capt Carl Dewey, and Gen Davenport Johnson. The general, resplendent in his dress blue uniform, spoke for the US Army Air Corps. Several hundred invited guests attended the ceremonies, but few family members of the cadets were present. The country was still in the grips of the depression. Few people could afford the trip from remote parts of the country even for such an important affair.

Gen Davenport Johnson, in his wisdom, spoke of the future and of our mission. "Time is of the essence," he said. "Our Air Force will be called upon to operate over much larger ranges than is the case in European operations today. If the United States should become involved in the present world turmoil and be forced to defend the Western Hemisphere, we must be able to reach out from our coastal frontiers to discover, locate, and destroy the enemy before he can get in striking distance of vital objectives within the United States."[5]

On that happy and peaceful night in Florida surrounded by the luxury and grandeur of the stately Biltmore Hotel and the music of the university band, General Johnson, even with a prophet's mind, could not have understood the significance of the event. In the months ahead, Charlie Lunn's 44 cadets would be navigating missions of inestimable significance. Passengers on their planes would include such luminaries as Sir Winston Churchill, Madame and Generalissimo Chiang Kai-shek, Presidents Herbert Hoover, Franklin D. Roosevelt, Harry S Truman, Dwight Eisenhower, and Lyndon Johnson, and Generals Douglas MacArthur, George C. Marshall, and Curtis E. LeMay.

Within one year, instead of defending our shores, many of us would be navigating across the world to "locate and destroy the enemy." Classmates would fly combat missions on every battlefront in World War II: in the frigid Aleutian Islands, across the sand-blown deserts of North Africa, in distant Rangoon, Saipan, and Germany. They would navigate on the first aerial attack on Japan and later with the B-29s burn Japanese cities. They would "seek out and destroy" V-1 and V-2 launching pads and submarine pens on the continent of Europe and help soften up the beaches of Normandy for the D day invasion. They would be prisoners of the Japanese and the Germans, and internees of the Turks. They would help in the project to dig the tunnel for the great escape from Stalag Luft III in Germany. They would travel the brutal Bataan Death March and lose classmates in the horrible Japanese prison camps.

At the commencement exercises of the celestial navigators of the Class of 40-A, General Johnson could have said, "These navigators will follow the stars on a path of tragedy and glory unique in the annals of American military history."

Notes

1. The Pan American-run school at Coral Gables was a short-run solution to the sudden and massive growth of demand for trained navigators in the Army Air Corps (AAC) (known after July 1941 as the Army Air Forces [AAF]). By late 1941, the AAF was meeting that demand with graduates from three navigation schools of its own located at Kelly Field, San Antonio, Texas; Mather Field, Sacramento, California; and Turner Field, Albany, Georiga. By the time the Japanese attacked Pearl Harbor, the Pan American facility at Coral Gables was largely given over to training fledgling navigators

for the Royal Air Force. The best scholarly account of aerial navigation down to World War II is Monte D. Wright, *Most Probable Position: A History of Aerial Navigation to 1941* (Lawrence, Kans.: University Press of Kansas, 1972). The relatively brief existence of the Pan American facility as a training school for AAC navigators is noted on page 189.

2. Army Air Forces, "Flying Training Command Historical Reviews," 1 January 1939–30 June 1946, held by Historical Research Agency, Maxwell AFB, Alabama.

3. Ibid. Prior to World War II, the Army Air Corps had no school dedicated to training aerial navigators and Monte Wright in *Most Probable Position*, 175, describes pre-World War II navigation training in the AAC as "neither lenghthy nor rigorous." In fact, specialized officer aircrew members were unknown in the prewar AAC and navigators, as a distinct group of rated aviators, simply did not exist. All flying officers were pilots, some of whom might be called upon to perform navigator functions. Aerial navigation was considered just another flying skill that some pilots were expected to master. The most ambitious AAC training program for pilot-navigators was instituted in 1933 when the 2d Bomb Group at Langley Field, Virginia, and the 7th Bomb Group at Rockwell Field, California, offered standardized navigation courses to pilots drawn from units across the Air Corps. The program was cancelled the following year, a casualty of limited resources and the Air Corps' costly involvement in government airmail operations. From 1934 until the establishment of the Pan American school at Coral Gables, navigation training reverted to individual units where it was conducted on a limited and more or less haphazard basis to meet local requirements.

4. Charles J. Lunn, interview with author, 1980; and Office of the Chief of the Air Corps to Dr B. F. Ashe, letter, subject: Pan American Navigation School, 24 July 1940.

5. Pan American Airways, Inc., *New Horizons*, New York, December 1940, 11.

Prelude to War

Upon graduation, I (Ed Whitcomb) was assigned to March Field at Riverside, California, along with 17 of my classmates. Eight class members were assigned as instructors at newly established Army Air Corps navigation schools. The other members were assigned to Fort Douglas near Salt Lake City, Utah.

From the moment we reached California, life took on new meaning. March Field opened up a world of exciting adventures for young officers who enjoyed peacetime life in the glamorous environment of southern California with nearby Hollywood and Palm Springs. The base was laid out beautifully with Spanish-style buildings on streets lined with tall palm trees. Landscaping seemed immaculate.

March Field was undoubtedly the most glamorous US military base. Army officers commonly were seen in company with movie celebrities while attending dances and other social functions at the Officers' Club. We were entertained by Bob Hope in his very first performance for the military forces. At another program, Tony Martin, a well-known singer, sang to the accompaniment of Jerome Kern, the great composer.

Though the navigators had a feeling that the US would soon become involved in combat, military duties were in the tradition of the peacetime Army. Excerpts from letters I wrote home to my mother illustrate the kind of life we led.

12 December 1940

Dear Mother,

We have been living a leisurely life up to now. We report to the squadron at 8:00 o'clock each morning and attend classes on an average of about an hour and a half a day.

19 December 1940

Have been working on a film with Warner Bros. Pictures for past two days as a technical advisor in a short that they are filming here "Wings of Steel. . . ." Last night they invited me to a big party at the old Mission Inn in Riverside.

2 February 1941

Movie actress Gail Patrick was there last night with one of my friends. Tyrone Power was over at the club yesterday afternoon while I was there. Next Sunday there is going to be a big blow-out at the club at which all of the Riverside Debs will be presented.

11 February 1941

I think that I told you that I had joined the Victoria Country Club. They have the prettiest golf courses there that I have ever seen in my life. The grass is so green and the snow capped mountains in the background make a beautiful picture. We have been playing just about every afternoon.

The high brass seemed oblivious to the fact that Japanese and German airmen, our most likely adversaries in the event of war, were flying daily combat missions against our potential allies. The most serious efforts of US bombardment crews at the time were conducting training missions which consisted of dropping bombs at targets on Muroc Dry Lake (later Edwards Air Force Base). For the most part, there were cloudless skies where visibility was unlimited and there were no enemy fighters or antiaircraft fire to distract the flight crews. All pilots were checked out as celestial navigators and expert bombardiers. To qualify as an expert bombardier, it was necessary to score as follows:

Altitude of flight	Permissible error
5,000 feet	75 feet
10,000 feet	150 feet
15,000 feet	225 feet

Gunnery practice for aircrews consisted of firing machine guns at a sleeve towed parallel to the line of flight of the gunners by an obsolete B-18 aircraft. These mock combat activities continued from November 1940 until April of 1941. Then conditions began to change as indicated by more letters home.

7 May 1941

Dear Mother,

For the first time since I have been here at March Field, I actually find myself so busy that I hardly have time to write. With 8 new Flying Fortresses in our squadron they have really kept us busy calibrating the instruments.

12 May 1941

Well this is the eve of one of the big moments in this dull life of mine. Cannot tell you; but I'm sure you will love it.

18 May 1941

This is Hawaii and it is great. We flew up to San Francisco last Tuesday morning. At 10:20 p.m. Indiana time, we passed over the southern tip of the Golden Gate Bridge and plunged into the darkest, blackest night you have ever seen. First, before we lost sight of the mass of lights of San Francisco and Oakland, powerful searchlights from the anti-aircraft batteries along the coast played on our planes bidding us a final farewell from the mainland.

We climbed through a rain squall which hung just out of San Francisco Bay and finally broke out into the clear at 10,000 feet to find our old friends, the stars, waiting to guide us across a couple thousand miles of water to our destination.

Our flight, as you may already know, was a mass armada of new Flying Fortresses which we were delivering to the Army here—the greatest mass flight the Army has ever made.

Next Tuesday we will be sailing home on the USS *Washington*. I understand it is one of the finest ships on the seas these days. I also understand that the wives and daughters from the Philippines are being returned to the States on the same boat.

28 May 1941

Aboard the USS *Washington* We heard FDR's speech last night. . . . Looks as if we are well on the way toward war. . . . This trip has put me closer to wartime conditions than I have ever been before with the war maneuvers in Hawaii and all of the refugees on this boat. In Hawaii the Air Corps was on 24-hour alert while we were there, and they were being called out at all hours of the night and day to perform mock battles.

On the trip back to the United States at a special meeting aboard the USS *Washington* all aircrew members were invited to volunteer for duty ferrying military aircraft from Canada to the Royal Air Force in England. All of the March Field crews volunteered, but few were called for ferry duty.

By the summer of 1941, the Japanese had been at war with China for more than four years in an effort to expand Japan's influence in the Far East. Newspapers and radio commentators reported that Japanese troops had crossed the border of Indochina. In July the US cut off oil shipments to Japan. The cutoff was serious because the Japanese were buying more than 50 percent of their petroleum products from the US. They needed gasoline and oil to carry on their military operation.

War clouds were gathering over the Western Pacific when Gen Henry ("Hap") Arnold, chief of the US Army Air Corps, ordered a study of the defenses of Oahu, the Hawaiian Island occupied by Pearl Harbor and the all important Hickam Field. The report delivered to the general in August 1941 was entitled, "Plan for the Employment of Bombardment Aviation in the Defense of Oahu." The report was uncanny. It predicted that the Japanese probably would employ a maximum of six aircraft carriers against Oahu. Then, as if by some premonition, on page five a statement was underlined for emphasis, "an early morning attack is therefore, the best plan of action to the enemy."[1]

The report also stated that a minimum of 36 B-17 bombers would be required to disable and destroy the aircraft carriers. The report recommended that 180 bombers be allocated to Hawaii immediately. We returned to our home station at March Field. Then in September 1941, just four months before the beginning of WWII, we were ordered to Albuquerque, New Mexico. There we made preparations for a special mission of the 19th Bombardment Group to go to the Philippine Islands.

The leader of the bombardment group was an outstanding aerial commander by the name of Col Eugene L. Eubank. Lean and erect, his first interest had to do with the welfare and military capabilities of the men in his command. At March Field he had been known to traipse from squadron to squadron checking on the navigational proficiency of his flying officers. He was concerned that his pilots as well as navigators knew celestial navigation.

His own background went deep into the history of the Air Corps. A member of the first class of flying cadets at Kelly Field, Texas, he remained as an instructor because of his outstanding ability as a flyer. That was even before he was commissioned as a second lieutenant. Later, he served as chief test pilot for the Air Corps Experimental Division at Dayton, Ohio. There he was friends with Orville Wright and Charles A. Lindbergh. Like them he was a true pioneer in aviation. After that he commanded the Institute of Technology at Fort Leavenworth, Kansas, before attending the Army's Command and General Staff School. Nobody was better qualified to lead the first US air unit into combat in WWII than the man we affectionately referred to as "Pappy" Eubank.

My next letter home was written aboard a new B-17D Flying Fortress as it approached Hawaii en route to the Philippine Islands.

18 October 1941

Dear Mother,

Oh, boy! Oh, boy! Oh, boy! There she is. Yep, old Hawaii just peeked over the horizon and you cannot imagine how happy I am about the whole thing. We have been in the air 12 hours now and in another hour we'll be bouncing into Hickam Field.

25 October 1941

This is Wake Island. We had a pleasant flight from Midway yesterday . . . tonight we will set sail for Port Moresby, New Guinea, better than a thousand miles below the equator. . . . By the time you get this, I should be in my new home in P.I. Hope it is a nice place to live.

Less than one year after Gen Davenport Johnson's speech at our graduation, 14 of us (Jay M. Horowitz, George Berkowitz, John W. Cox, Harry J. Schreiber, Walter E. Seamon, Jr., William F. Meenagh, Anthony E. Oliver, Harold C. McAuliff, George M. Markovich, Jack E. Jones, Arthur E. Hoffman, Charles J. Stevens, William S. Warner, and I) were far from America's "coastal frontiers." We were on Clark Field in the Philippine Islands, 7,000 miles from United States shores.

Each of us had navigated the broad Pacific Ocean from San Francisco via Hawaii, Midway Island, Wake Island, Port Moresby, and Port Darwin. It was a glorious flight virtually without incident. We had used all the procedures and techniques that Charlie Lunn had taught us and developed some of our own. The trip was the greatest mass flight of aircraft in history up to that time. Our 26 shiny new B-17 Flying Fortresses fresh from the Boeing factory in Seattle brought the strength of heavy bombers at Clark Field to 35.

> Manila Hotel
>
> 1 November 1941
>
> We have been here (Philippines) several days and have found the place a nice place to live. From the hotel window here where I am writing, I have a beautiful view across a golf course to the walled city of old Manila.
>
> We don't know when this war will begin and no-one seems to care a lot. . . . You probably know a lot more about what's happening than we do. . . . Before you get this I'll be 24.

> 21 November 1941
>
> We don't have any more idea what might happen here than the next guy. All I know is that they seem to be preparing for the worst with boatload after boatload of planes, tanks, fuel, and men arriving all the time. Heard yesterday that three more squadrons of bombers were due to arrive.

The new environment in the Philippines was a world apart from anything we had ever known. It was November 1941, and the threat of war was in the air. Everyone knew that but there was little or no talk about what it would be like if war erupted. Sometimes I tried to visualize what it would be like in the Flying Fortress high up in "the Wild Blue Yonder." There would be enemy aircraft firing machine-gun bullets at the plane and enemy antiaircraft shells coming at us. I suspected and hoped that our planes would fly so fast and so high that no enemy planes or antiaircraft fire could reach us. I did not know that for a fact because there was no experience upon which to base such a judgment. To my knowledge it was a matter that other crew members did not discuss.

Never before in the history of our country had we used heavy bombardment planes against an enemy. There were many things that we did not know. One thing that we did know was that war with Japan was near. Yet when war would erupt was vague in our minds. It seemed remote to the point of being unreal that such a thing would happen.

We all knew of the exploits of Capt Eddie Rickenbacker and others in World War I. That was a long time ago and a different kind of war. This war would not be like the aerial warfare of World War I. Our planes would have a crew made up of specialists including pilots, navigator, bombardier, crew chief, radio operator, and gunners. Besides having the newest and finest of heavy bombers, we had the supersecret Norden Bomb Sight. Rumor said that it was so accurate that the bombardier could drop a bomb in a pickle barrel from 20,000 feet. We also knew that our pilots were the finest in the world because of the high standards of qualification and training in the United States Army Air Corps.

We gave little thought to the fact that Japanese pilots and aircrew members were seasoned veterans in aerial warfare. Our position was different. Not one of us had ever been on a real, live bombing mission or engaged in any aerial warfare against an enemy.

While we were getting acquainted with our new environ-ment, Maj Gen Lewis H. Brereton, General MacArthur's newly assigned air commander, called all the aircrew members together for a meeting at the base theater. There he told us that the international condition had grown worse and that we might be involved in war as early as April 1942.

There were grandiose plans for beefing up the aerial strength of the Philippines because the War Department was committed to an all-out effort to strengthen the air defenses of the islands. With all the good intentions, the air defense turned out to be a matter of much too little, much too late. War was much nearer than anyone had expected. We would soon learn whether our mighty B-17s would fly higher and faster than any Japanese planes and whether our supersecret bomb sight would live up to its reputation.

On the night of 6 December 1941 more new B-17s were on their way from Salt Lake City to join us in the Philippines.

Navigating the planes were Louis G. Moslener, Jr., Richard Wellington Cease, Merrill K. Gordon, George A. Walthers, Robert A. Trenkle, Paul E. Dawson, and Russell M. Vifquain, Jr., but not one of them reached the Philippines. The following chapters relate their stories.

Notes

1. *Hearings before the Joint Committee on the Investigation of the Pearl Harbor Attack,* 79th Cong., 1946, 33/883 (unpublished).

Death on a Bright
Sunday Morning

The Army Air Corps assigned Louis G. Moslener, Jr., to Fort Douglas near Salt Lake City, Utah after graduation from navigation school. Accompanying him on that assignment were his classmates, Fredrick T. Albanese, Robert T. Arnoldus, Charles G. Benes, Carroll F. Cain, Richard W. Cease, Melvin Cobb, Paul E. Dawson, Jr., Merrill K. Dawson, Jr., Edmund A. Koterwas, Edward L. Marsh, Leroy L. Tempest, Barry P. Thompson, Robert A. Trenkle, Russell M. Vifquain, Jr., George A. Walthers, and James F. Wilson. In Salt Lake City, Moslener took quarters off the military base in the home of Mrs Margaret Powell. Joining him there was Richard Cease, a fellow Pennsylvanian from Trucksville in the eastern part of the state near Wilkes-Barre. Moslener's hometown was Monaca, a small town north of Pittsburgh.

The genial Mrs Powell made her residence a home away from home for "her boys." But the homelike environment was not for long because secret order code name "Plum" called for the movement of a large number of heavy bombers to the Philippine Islands. All available navigators would be needed to guide them across the sea.

On 5 December 1941 at the first light of dawn a tiny, dark mound pushed up from the distant horizon across the water. It was a welcome sight for Louis G. Moslener, Jr., because he was navigating on his first long, overwater flight. As a member of a crew of 11 airmen, he was on his way to the Philippine Islands. The long trip would take him to the romantic islands of Hawaii. For almost 12 hours the big B-17 Flying Fortress had been plowing through the black of night about 8,000 feet above the Pacific Ocean.

I knew the trip well because I had made it twice. Louis would have been weary from the long night of seeking out stars, taking celestial fixes and plotting them on his chart. Sometimes the stars would have been elusive and would seem to dance in the field of vision of his octant. At other times, they would be blotted out by a cloud in the middle of taking an observation. Then there had been times when the turbulence of the air caused the plane to be so unsteady that celestial observations were difficult and even impossible. He had overcome the elements and felt good because that little hump on the horizon told him that his navigation had been accurate. The flight was approaching Hawaii, the first stop on their way to the Philippines. Later a couple more mounds appeared on the distant edge of the ocean. He was able to identify them as the islands of Maui and Oahu. His destination was Hickam Field on the island of Oahu adjacent to the giant naval base of Pearl Harbor.

As the sun rose behind them, it became a bright sunny morning. It was an exhilarating feeling for Louis as his B-17 descended toward the island of Oahu and his pilot, Ted S. Faulkner, prepared for landing at Hickam Field. Louis hurriedly folded his navigational charts and packed away his equipment so he could drink up the scenery spread out before him. In a matter of seconds the plane would be on the ground.

The navigator's compartment, being in the plexiglas nose of the aircraft, gave the young navigator a panoramic view of the beautiful island and everything on it. He saw the white rim of the waves lapping lazily along the shore and hills green with tropical foliage. Then there were the long runways of Hickam Field and the giant Navy base at Pearl Harbor clogged with warships. Hawaii was a beautiful and exciting place that sunny morning.

Moslener knew that there was a great urgency for getting B-17 bombers to the Philippine Islands. There had been little advance notice, but he was well prepared and ready. He did not know that relations between the US and Japan had reached an impasse or that Japanese warships were steaming toward Pearl Harbor even as his plane was descending toward Hickam Field.

By a strange quirk of fate, the Japanese admiral who masterminded the attack did not favor going to war against the United States. Japanese extremists hated Admiral Isoroku Yamamoto and considered him pro-American. He had attended Harvard University, served as a naval attaché in Washington, D.C., and had regularly attended American

League baseball games at Griffith Stadium in Washington, D.C. He had a healthy respect for American war potential.

In compliance with Admiral Yamamoto's plan, six aircraft carriers were steaming toward Hawaii at the time Moslener's plane was landing. The wheels of the plane touched the ground and the first leg of the long flight had been successful. The crew was safe in the romantic Hawaiian Islands. But there would be little time to visit. After a rest and inspection of the aircraft, the crew would be moving on to Midway, Wake Island, and the Philippines.

Then came Sunday morning. If he were back home in Monaca, Pennsylvania, Moslener would have been getting ready for Sunday school at the Presbyterian Church with his mother and father. He had not been able to tell them that he was on the way to the Philippines because of the secrecy of the mission.

A few days earlier he had written to them telling them that he was "going on a long journey." Then he had added, "but please don't worry." In his mind there was nothing to worry about because he knew that many of us had made the trip to the Philippines safely. However, his parents did worry as all parents worry about their children in military service.

People in Monaca knew Moslener's father well. He was a civil engineer and president of the local public school board. When people in the community asked about young Louis, his father was happy to tell them that Louis was a 2d lieutenant in the Air Corps and a navigator on a B-17 bomber. Although Louis had earned his wings in the Air Corps, his friends and neighbors could not think of him that way. They remembered him only as the skinny, blond-headed young fellow who had been active in church work, in the Young People's Forum, the DeMolay, and in the high school band. It was hard for them to relate the young boy they had known to a six-foot, 160-pound, 23-year-old officer in the Army Air Corps.

Early Sunday morning on 7 December Moslener and his crew met at hangar 15 at Hickam Field. They were there to take their plane on a short check flight before the next leg of their long journey. Without any warning there was a terrific bomb explosion near the corner of the hangar next to the

23

railroad track. The crew members except Moslener scattered seeking protection. Moslener lay dead on the hangar floor.

Just 48 hours before the bomb fell his mother and father had opened the letter from Louis saying Louis was "going on a long journey." The next message his parents received was a letter from his commanding officer, Maj Richard H. Carmichael (later Major General), saying

> Men died and are dying that peace may be the lot of those they love. One of the men who gave his life in the sudden attack here on the morning of December 7th was your son, Louis Gustav. He was killed instantly by the first bomb dropped by the Japanese in this war.[1]

World War II had begun for the United States. Louis G. Moslener was the first but not the last of our classmates to make the supreme sacrifice for his country.

Notes

1. *The Dallas Post*, Dallas, Pennsylvania, Friday, 3 April 1942.

Attack on Clark Field

Several hours passed after the attack on Pearl Harbor before US personnel stationed in Clark Field learned of the Japanese attack. Along with other crew members, I (Ed Whitcomb) showered, dressed, and headed out into the sunshine of a bright new Monday morning. I was on the way to breakfast at the mess hall a block away. It seemed that it would be just another day of preparing to go to war until somebody said, "There is a rumor that the Japanese attacked Pearl Harbor."

Following that there was some discussion ridiculing the idea. It made no sense whatsoever. US bases in the Philippines were much closer to Japan than Hawaii. Why would the Japanese attack Pearl Harbor and leave Philippine bases with their fleet of bombers ready to attack the island of Formosa?

Then we heard a radio from one of the nearby barracks. It was Don Bell, the well-known voice of the news from Manila, reporting, "The Japanese have bombed Pearl Harbor!"

We had no way of knowing of the extensive damage the Japanese had inflicted upon Pearl Harbor; nor did we know that our friend and classmate, Louis Moslener, had been a victim of that attack. I went directly to the 19th Group Headquarters. It was an old two-story frame building facing the airfield where I had spent most of my time since our arrival in the islands. My job had been sorting maps and taking inventory of our navigation equipment.

Our commander, Col Eugene L. Eubank, had learned of the attack on Pearl Harbor early in the morning. He had rushed to Manila to seek permission for us to carry out a bombing mission on the Japanese airfields on Formosa, 500 miles to the north. It seemed strange that he needed to ask for permission. We could not understand why we could not attack the enemy. We waited for the colonel's return. In the meantime everything was at a standstill in headquarters. My most important priority appeared to be to get to the mess hall. It might be a long time before we would have another chance for a decent meal. I hurried along the long, tree-lined walk to the mess hall. Across the field our planes were poised and ready to go. We could be in our B-17s in two minutes when we got word to go. We were ready.

Flyers crowded the mess hall to enjoy generous portions of breakfast with tall glasses of pineapple or orange juice or whatever a person cared to eat or drink. After a hurried meal, I anxiously made my way back to the headquarters.

There pilot Edwin Green asked me to make certain that our B-17 cameras contained film for an aerial reconnaissance mission. A driver delivered me to the plane in seconds. Seeing that there was no film, I hurried to a supply tent within easy walking distance and picked up the film after first signing the appropriate receipt. However, when I stepped outside the tent, I discovered that my plane had taken off! It seemed to have vanished almost before my eyes! I learned that during the short time I had been in the supply tent, a field alert caused almost all flyable planes to leave the ground.

Back at headquarters, I busied myself sorting maps until Colonel Eubank returned from Manila and called a meeting. We assembled on the street in front of the headquarters building at about 1030. There the colonel reported the bewildering news that he had been unable to get authority to fly a bombing mission. He had gone to the headquarters of Maj Gen Lewis H. Brereton, commander of the Far East Air Force (FEAF).* General Brereton, the top Air Corps officer in the Philippines, had not been able to see General MacArthur. Brereton talked to Gen Richard K. Sutherland, MacArthur's chief of staff, who ordered three B-17s to fly reconnaissance missions to Formosa but did not authorize a bombing mission.

Still nothing happened. We waited and speculated. We had no way of knowing that fog covered the airfields at Formosa that morning, nor did we know that there were some 600 planes on the ground there. Had we been able to fly a recon-naissance mission to Formosa that morning, it is certain that we would have received a warm and overwhelming reception.

---

*Brereton's FEAF consisted of approximately 316 aircraft, over two-thirds of them obsolete. His complement of first-line combat planes consisted of 35 B-17s and 90 P-40s.

The long worrisome morning whiled away and again I hurried to the mess hall for a quick meal. As I departed the hall, George Berkowitz, a classmate and fellow navigator, was just coming in for lunch. He reported that nothing had changed at headquarters.

Suspense filled the air, yet we felt helpless. There was no question that America was at war. We all wanted to fly. We were ready.

There was no warning at headquarters of Japanese planes approaching Clark Field. Despite all our warning systems and all the reconnaissance missions we had flown, the Japanese caught us by surprise. The first notice we had at the 19th Bombardment Group Headquarters was when someone screamed, "Here they come!"

At that moment, the bombs were on their way. I dove into a trench about 30 feet to the rear of the headquarters building. Explosions rocked the ground and sent shock waves through my body. Other bodies crushed me to the dark bottom of the trench until my face and body pushed into the pounding earth. The explosions continued and the earth seemed to heave with each blast. We learned later that there had been two waves of 27 high-flying bombers each. Bombs hit the officers' mess hall, many planes on the flight line, and the hangar area. At the time I did not know that Berkowitz had suffered disaster as he left the mess hall.

When the bombers had done their damage and departed, we started to extricate our bodies from the trench. Then the staccato sound of machine-gun fire shattered the air. We quickly realized that Zero fighters were strafing the field. Back and forth they flew, time after time, raking the field and the hangar line with their deadly fire. Huge black clouds from burning planes and the fuel supply dump blotted out the noonday sun as the planes continued their destruction virtually unopposed.

With grime in my ears, eyes, nose, and mouth, I struggled to get out of the trench when the strafing ended. The bombing and strafing attacks had been a terrorizing ordeal. I was so shaken that for a time I was uncertain of my own physical condition. The crackling sound of burning filled the air along with intermittent explosions from the direction of the flight line. I found Colonel Eubank beside the headquarters building. He was witnessing the destruction of half of his bomber fleet.[1]

Just as I was ready to set out for the flight line to see the damage to our planes, another flight of fighters streaked in across the field at treetop level. They were so low that the Japanese pilots were plainly visible. Colonel Eubank did not take cover. He stood helplessly watching the enemy planes darting in and out, spraying the field with their devastating fire and destroying the remainder of his B-17s on the field. When the last Zero finally departed the area, Clark Field lay in ruins and the raid had killed more than 100 people.

We had considered Clark Field to be at the very forefront if we were to be forced to undertake an aerial offensive against the Japanese. Just two days before the Japanese raid, it had been the proud home of 35 of the world's finest bombardment aircraft. Fortunately, at the time of the attack, 16 bombers had moved to Del Monte Field on the island of Mindanao more than 500 miles to the south. They were beyond the range of the Japanese bombers based on Formosa and there was reason to believe that the Japanese were unaware of existence of Del Monte Field. At any rate, the 16 planes at Del Monte were safe from destruction on that disastrous first day of the war in the Pacific.

For weeks after the beginning of the war, the dirt airstrip at Del Monte became the most important base for air operations in the islands. Most of the aircrew members who reached Del Monte Field were able to fly to Australia and avoid the prison camp life that many of us suffered in the months ahead.[2]

Notes

1. The first wave of Formosa-based Japanese planes (54 bombers and 36 Zero fighters) attacked Clark Field at approximately 1220 on 8 December 1941. Although nine hours had elapsed since MacArthur's headquarters had received news of the disastrous events at Pearl Harbor, American forces at Clark were no better prepared than those in Hawaii for a Japanese raid. During the 30-minute attack, virtually every building on the base was destroyed or damaged, and hundreds of people were killed or wounded. Flights of Zeros made multiple strafing passes as the bombers departed. Only four P-40s managed to get airborne in a hopeless effort to engage the high-flying Japanese bomber force. Virtually every B-17 on the base—two squadrons' worth—was either destroyed or badly shot up. The same fate befell an entire squadron of P-40 fighters.

Exactly what transpired in the discussions on the hectic morning of 8 December between General MacArthur, his chief of staff, Maj Gen Richard K. Sutherland, and Major General Brereton, has never been resolved. All three men later gave conflicting accounts. What does seem clear is that over a five- or six-hour period, Brereton made three attempts to see MacArthur, presumably to gain permission to launch a preemptive B-17 raid against Japanese air bases in Formosa. In each case, the imperious Sutherland denied Brereton access to MacArthur. Sometime between ten and eleven A.M. Brereton finally received the directive he sought. By 1120, orders to arm and fuel the B-17s had been teletyped to Clark Field, but the American bombers were still on the ground when the Japanese planes appeared overhead an hour later. Whether or not commanders at Clark Field received adequate advance notice about the inbound Japanese force also remains in dispute.

Altogether, over the next four days, the Japanese conducted 14 major air raids against various military and naval sites in the Manila and Clark areas. Always outnumbered, the FEAF steadily lost more planes as aircrews mounted a desperate series of air defense efforts.

For a detailed account of the debacle at Clark Field, see Wesley Frank Craven and James Lea Cate, eds., *The Army Air Forces in World War II*, vol. 1, *Plans and Early Operations, January 1939 to August 1942* (Chicago: University of Chicago Press, 1948–58), 203–10. A judicious appraisal of the disaster is in D. Clayton James, *The Years of MacArthur, 1941–1945*, vol. 2 (Boston: Houghton Mifflin, 1975), 5–15. Shorter and more recent summaries are in Ronald H. Spector, *Eagle Against the Sun: The American War with Japan* (New York: Free Press, 1985), 106–8, and Geoffrey Perret, *Winged Victory: The Army Air Forces in World War II* (New York: Random House, 1993), 78–81. General Brereton's recollections of this event are in Lewis H. Brereton, *The Brereton Diaries: The War in the Air in the Pacific, Middle East and Europe, 3 October 1941–8 May 1945* (New York: William Morrow, 1946).

2. Del Monte Field was an unimproved landing strip on a narrow plateau adjoining the Del Monte Corporation's pineapple plantation on the northern shore of the island of Mindanao. Since Del Monte Field lacked landing aids and was surrounded by 4,000 mountains, landing a B-17 at Del Monte in darkness or bad weather constituted a test of skill and nerve even for seasoned Fortress pilots. In anticipation of eventually basing his entire heavy bomber fleet on Mindanao, General Brereton had sent two B-17 squadrons (16 aircraft) and a small number of B-18s to Del Monte in early December 1941. The anticipated eminent arrival of the entire 7th Bomb Group at little Del Monte limited the number of planes Brereton could deploy from Clark Field. Craven and Cate, 187–89. Landing a B-17 at Del Monte under adverse conditions is characterized as a "white-knuckle" experience in Perret, 78–79.

George Berkowitz

If there had been a designation of a Mr Congeniality in the Class of 40-A, it surely would have gone to George Bernard Berkowitz. He was a happy-go-lucky navigator from Dallas and the University of Texas. George was unquestionably the most colorful and popular member of the class. He was a big, well-proportioned 175-pound fellow. His 6'2" frame was topped off by a crop of sandy hair with a reddish tinge. A few freckles were randomly sprinkled across his face. He liked well-tailored clothes and big cigars.

The scowl on George's face belied the fact that the imps of devilment were dancing in his head. He was totally undependable in conversation. In the middle of a serious discussion he might pull out a big cigar, light it, and turn on his heels with a comment like, "Don't bother me now. Can't you see I have a lot of important things on my mind?"

Those of us who knew him knew that it was all in jest and in the nature of an act he played continually. With him it was always the unexpected. He might borrow money from a friend then take him out to dinner. However, he was prompt to repay his debts on payday.

On one occasion when his plane was high over the western Pacific, Saint Elmo's fire enveloped his aircraft. That is a condition when a fiery glow develops over the exterior of the plane while in flight. It is temporary and not dangerous. Being unfamiliar with it, Berkowitz became alarmed. It alarmed Berkowitz until his pilot, Col Bert Cosgrove, explained the phenomenon to him.

In mock seriousness Berkowitz asked, "Can you tell me where I can catch the first bus back to Dallas?" With all his eccentricity, George was serious about his job as a navigator. Like other members of our class, he had successfully brought his bomber across the Pacific. Since then we had been in the Philippines learning about life in the Orient and getting prepared for war.

George was having a hurried lunch in the officers' mess hall where I (Ed Whitcomb) had eaten just 15 minutes earlier. The officers about him engaged in lighthearted banter concerning the report of a Japanese attack on Pearl Harbor. Why would they attack Pear Harbor and ignore Clark Field which had a fleet of the finest bombers in the world supported by squadrons of fighter planes? It had been almost seven hours since they had first heard the rumor, yet nothing had happened at Clark Field. There had been that false alarm of enemy planes approaching the field. Our planes had taken to the skies, but no one had sighted any hostile planes. Our airplanes returned to the base and were waiting for further orders. The situation was confusing. No one could understand why we had not been ordered to fly a bombing mission.

Then abruptly the mood changed. A mighty bomb blast rocked the mess hall followed by the roar of more and more earth-shaking blasts. The mess hall had received a direct hit. Panic set in. Flyers rushed for the door, some heading directly across the field to the flight line two blocks away. There was screaming and moaning of civilian workers and officers who had been struck by bomb fragments.

Berkowitz was running across the field to his plane when a large chunk of bomb fragment chopped him down. In a state of excruciating pain and semiconsciousness, he realized that others had been hit by bomb fragments. Then a second wave of the high-flying bombers laid a second pattern of bombs across the field. Buildings and planes were ablaze. After the bombers had passed, fighter planes raked the field at treetop level darting in and out of the black columns of smoke from burning planes and the fuel dump.

As George lay on the ground, he became aware that his leg was mangled between the knee and the hip. He grew weak from the loss of blood and feared that he would die before help reached him. He screamed for help, but his voice was drowned out by the noise of explosions and machine-gun fire.

At long last stretcher bearers appeared. They loaded him into a vehicle and transported him to the nearby Fort Stotsenberg Hospital. There, in his faint condition, he received the devastating word that his leg would be amputated between the hip and the knee. There was no opportunity to ask questions. In his dismal state of mind he wondered what had happened? Did he really have to lose his leg? Where were his other crew members and his friends? What had happened to them? What would happen to him? Where was he going? He had no way of knowing.

Later George was moved by railroad car to the Philippine Women's University in Manila 56 miles away. Under other circumstances, he would have welcomed that environment. At that time the university had converted its facilities into a hospital for wounded soldiers. It was hoped that they could be moved out of the war zone, possibly to Australia. The only women Berkowitz saw at the Philippine Women's University were the busy Catholic sisters who kindly administered to the needs of the injured patients.

George languished in the hospital for three weeks, while the Japanese continued bombing and strafing the city about him. Then one afternoon there came a surprise for George. He looked up to see the smiling face of his commander, Col Eugene Eubank. The colonel had learned about him and had come to comfort him. It was then that George learned what had happened to his friends on that first day of the war.

Finally 248 wounded soldiers were moved through the streets of Manila to the dock area. Col Carlos Romalo of General MacArthur's staff had finally secured an ancient interisland steamer called the *Mactan*, which the Army converted into a hospital ship for evacuating wounded soldiers from the war zone. George and the other wounded embarked on the 46-year-old ship for the 2,000-mile ocean voyage to Australia. The crew had painted a big white cross on each side of the ship and the Red Cross flag hung from the main halyards. As the *Mactan* left the docks, those on the upper decks could see huge fires burning supply dumps and lighting up the skyline of Manila.

On New Year's Eve 1941, the *Mactan* sailed out of Manila Bay between the peninsula of Bataan and the island of Corregidor. It then made its way through the mine fields about Corregidor and headed south through Japanese-controlled waters. On the sixth day out, a series of blasts of the ship's whistle told the passengers that they were crossing the equator. Then came the Dutch Celebes and the Makassar Strait.

On the 18th day after they had left Manila, Radio Tokyo announced that the *Mactan* had been sunk and that there were no survivors. Had the report been true, George Berkowitz would have had a short war. He had envisioned navigating his bomber on high-altitude missions against the enemy. That had all ended before it had begun. His mighty bomber was no more than a heap of molten metal back at Clark Field where George had lost his leg on the first day of the war.

Many radio listeners in the southwest Pacific believed the Radio Tokyo broadcast. Only those aboard the *Mactan* knew for certain that the broadcast was only false Japanese propaganda. They laughed an uneasy laugh about it until they were safely ashore in Sydney, Australia, after stops at Darwin, Townsville, and Brisbane. The *Mactan* docked at Sidney on 27 January 1942.

George was moved from Sidney to a hospital in Melbourne. There he felt very much alone and far away from the war and far away from his friends in the 19th Bombardment Group. What would happen to him next? What had happened to all the friends he had left behind? Those questions plagued his mind as he lay recovering from his injury.

News reports indicated that things were going badly for General MacArthur's forces in the Philippines. Only Bataan, the tiny island of Corregidor, and some scattered forces on the southern island of Mindanao had survived the onslaught of the Japanese forces. George endured long and difficult days recuperating in a foreign hospital far from family and friends.

Then came word that the 19th Bombardment Group headquarters had evacuated the Philippines just 10 days after George had been injured. It was operating out of northern Australia and Java. Many members of the organization were missing in action or dead in the Philippines. After George recovered his strength, he requested orders to go back to his outfit. That request was denied and he returned to the United States. But George Berkowitz was not one to be counted out of the war so early.

Undaunted in spirit he was fitted with an artificial leg. Then he applied for and received special permission from General Hap Arnold to continue in the Air Corps as a navigation instructor for the duration of the war. He remained active as a navigation instructor in Texas until his retirement.

Harry Schreiber

Four days after the first attack on Clark Field, US planes observed unusual naval activity at a port about 200 miles southeast of Manila. Japanese transports protected by naval craft were unloading cargo and troops at the port city of Legaspi. The 19th Bombardment Group Headquarters ordered a raid by planes from Del Monte Field against the port.[1]

Six Fortresses were to fly in close formation for their mutual protection. Fighter escort was not available. During the mission only three planes were able to reach the target area. Navigating two of those three planes were Harry Schreiber and William Meenagh. Meenagh's plane developed engine trouble and dropped out of the formation shortly after takeoff. Nevertheless, it continued to the target alone.

As Harry Schreiber's plane approached Legaspi at 18,000 feet, the crew saw a large concentration of warships in the harbor. They also saw many Japanese fighters taking off from aircraft carriers.

Immediately after Schreiber's plane dropped its bombs, the fighters swarmed up after the plane. Jack Adams, the pilot, dove the plane into the clouds at about 8,000 feet. Machine-gun bullets ripped through the thin skin of the B-17 plane as five Zeros closed in. Machine gunners on Schreiber's plane shot four of the intruders down in flames. Nevertheless, the fighters had done their damage. Enemy fire knocked out two engines on the B-17 and wounded one of the crew members. It was clear that the crew would have to bail out or crash-land the plane.

With an island in sight ahead, the pilot decided to crash-land. While Adams was maneuvering for a landing, the crew observed the one remaining fighter still coming after them. There was nothing they could do but ride the plane down to the crash landing. Adams skillfully guided the plane to a wheels-up landing, and it skidded to a stop. Crew members scampered from the ship to find protection from the oncoming fighter. The one member of the crew who did not get out of the downed plane was the copilot. He sat in the cockpit in a dazed condition, unscathed, as machine-gun bullets peppered all about him. The Japanese pilot, satisfied that he had made his kill, headed back to Legaspi. When the crew returned to their wrecked plane, the copilot was waiting for them and wondering what had happened.

As the crew members were trying to determine their next move, they faced a new problem. Suddenly a group of angry Filipinos brandishing machetes surrounded them. The natives had mistaken the crew for Japanese and were ready to attack them. In a short time, the flyers convinced the Filipinos that they were Americans. At that point, the Filipinos became very friendly and helpful. Quickly they transported the crew members to a town where they could get medical attention. There a doctor removed a cannon round from the leg of the injured crew member. It was then they learned that they were on the Philippine Island of Masbate.

After a week, the crew purchased an outrigger canoe for 50 pesos and hired a native to sail them to the island of Panay. There the Philippine Army conscripted the officers into the guerilla forces. At first, most of the officers were in awe of the responsibility of their assignments for they were to be battalion commanders in the Philippine Field Artillery. Schreiber had completed four years of Reserve Officer Training Corps (ROTC) at Texas A&M; so he felt confident that he could handle the assignment.

When the time came to meet their respective commands, the Americans were dismayed. They learned that instead of a normal battalion strength of 1,000 troops, their commands consisted of only a couple of hundred high school age boys. Most of them could not speak or understand English. Each boy had a rifle and approximately 15 rounds of ammunition. The only connection the outfit had with the field artillery was that it had six sights from World War I French 75-millimeter field guns. Divers had salvaged the sights from the bottom of Manila Bay, and the Filipinos had polished the sights so that they glistened in the bright sunlight. The sights were the Filipinos' proudest possessions.

Faced with such an impossible situation, the aircrew officers were quick to desert their new high command positions and tried to find their way back to the remnants of the 19th Bombardment Group at Del Monte Field. They made their move in early January 1942. Upon reaching the city of Cagayan near Del Monte Field, they took assignments on beach defense duty until early March. Then they moved to Del Monte where many 19th Bomb Group crew members had been stranded for weeks waiting for transportation to Australia. Planes that could have moved them were busy flying raids in an effort to stop the Japanese move toward Australia.

In the meantime, the war in the Philippines had gone so badly that President Roosevelt ordered Gen Douglas MacArthur to abandon the Philippines. He and his party were making their way by PT boat from the island of Corregidor to Del Monte Field. There he would be transported by plane to Australia.

At about nine o'clock on the night of 13 March 1942, Schreiber was heartened to hear the engines of a B-17 as he and the crew waited at Del Monte Field. The field lights were turned on, but the plane disappeared in the blackness of the night. What they did not know was that it was Lt Henry Godman's plane. He had flown from Australia to rescue General MacArthur and his party, but he had been unable to see the lights of Del Monte Field. In attempting to let down out over the water the plane crashed. Lieutenant Godman nearly lost his life, but he prayed and promised the Lord that if he lived he would spend the rest of his life serving the Lord. He did survive, and, true to his commitment, he spent the remainder of his life in the Lord's service as an international officer in the Full Gospel Businessmens organization.

A couple hours after the sounds of Godman's plane faded into the night, the waiting crew members heard another plane. This time it was Lt Harl Pease. He was piloting another one of the four B-17s headquarters had ordered to Del Monte to transport General MacArthur and his party to Australia. Upon landing his plane, Pease learned that General MacArthur had not yet arrived from Corregidor. It might be several days before his arrival.

The following morning, Lieutenant Pease convinced the commander at Del Monte Field that his plane was in a bad state of repair and unsuitable for transporting the general and his party. Pease knew that his B-17 would not be safe sitting on the airfield during the daylight hours because enemy planes were attacking the field daily. Pease departed Del Monte Field for Australia early the next morning. He left without General MacArthur but with Harry Schreiber and 15 other aircrew members including Charles J. Stevens, another classmate from the Class of 40-A.

After continually running from Japanese forces, Schreiber was happy to be in Australia. He outfitted himself with a fresh khaki uniform and a complete new set of navigational equipment to replace those he had lost. The good news was that pilot Frank Kurtz selected Schreiber to be navigator on the personal aircraft of Gen George H. Brett, commander of the US Air Corps in Australia. His personal plane was a war-weary B-17D, which the crew had dubbed *Alexander the Swoose*. The general took it out of service as a combat plane to use for administrative flying. It was used to transport the general and other "high brass" in Australia and to the combat zone in New Guinea.[2]

On one such mission, Schreiber was navigating for General Brett, three other generals, some top Australian military officials, and a lanky former Texas congressman. The flight was to be from Port Darwin to the city of Cloncurry 800 miles to the southeast. When his chronometer told him that he had reached his estimated time of arrival (ETA), Schreiber scanned the open range of northern Australia without seeing any sign of a city. He was uncomfortable and red-faced when pilot Kurtz resorted to flying rectangular search patterns in hopes of locating Cloncurry. Finally upon sighting some farm buildings, Kurtz brought the 25-ton bomber down in an open field. The reason for the error in navigation was due to a malfunction of the octant. When asked later about Schreibers ability as a navigator, Kurtz commented that Schreiber was the best in the business.[3]

A short time after they landed, several curious sheep ranchers gathered about the plane. They had seen airplanes in the distant skies but were surprised to see a big four-engine bomber on the ground in their field. In no time the lanky Texan was out of the plane, shaking hands and talking to the ranchers on a first-name basis. They discussed the inequity of the high tariff on Australian wool and other subjects of interest to the ranchers. It was said that before the plane took to the skies again, the future president of the United States, Lyndon B. Johnson, had the votes of the northern Australian sheep ranchers in his hip pocket.[4]

Stepping back to March 1942 in the Philippines, Gen Douglas MacArthur was irate when he arrived at Del Monte Field and learned there was no plane to take him to Australia. As mentioned earlier, the plane that had brought Schreiber to Australia was one of the planes intended for the general. He and his party waited for three more days before another plane arrived to rescue them. Reports circulated that MacArthur blamed General Brett for that inconvenience and never forgave him. He soon assigned Gen George C. Kenney to Brett's job and sent Brett, Capt Frank Kurtz, and navigator Harry Schreiber back to the US for reassignment.

The war weary *Alexander the Swoose* made the trip from Australia to Washington, D.C., in 36 hours, breaking three speed records in the process. Later the B-17 became the property of the Smithsonian Institution in Washington, D.C. It remains there as the sole relic of the tragic and futile attempt by a few very brave airmen to stem the tide of the mighty Japanese war machine as it swept across the southwest Pacific to the doorsteps of Australia.

Notes

1. Legaspi is located on the southeast coast of Luzon. The Japanese landed some 3,000 men on the shore of Legaspi Bay on 12 December 1941. The B-17 raid to which the author refers was flown two days later. Although two B-17s were destroyed, the Japanese forces sustained no serious losses. Following this disappointing encounter, FEAFs remaining flyable B-17s departed the Philippines for Batchelor Field, Australia. Wesley Frank Craven and James Lea Cate, eds., *The Army Air Forces in World War II*, vol. 1, *Plans and Early Operations, January 1939 to August 1942* (Chicago: University of Chicago Press, 1948–1958), 219–22; Geoffrey Perret, *Winged Victory: The Army Air Forces in World War II* (New York: Random House, 1993), 80.

2. Maj Gen (later Lt Gen) George H. Brett was named commander of United States Army Forces in Australia (USAFIA) in late December 1941. Following MacArthurs arrival in Australia in March 1942, General Brett served as the first commander of Allied Air Forces, Southwest Pacific Area (SWPA). He was replaced as MacArthurs air commander in August 1942 by Lt Gen George C. Kenney. Craven and Cate, 326; and Perret, 166–69.

3. Frank Kurtz, interview with author, Hollywood, Calif., 1994.

4. In June 1942, Texas congressman Lyndon B. Johnson, then serving as a lieutenant commander in the US Navy Reserve, participated as President Franklin D. Roosevelt's personal representative in a War Department fact-finding mission to MacArthur's Southwest Pacific Theater command. Johnson's trip is briefly described in Perret, 165–66.

William Meenagh

Another navigator on that fateful Legaspi mission with Harry Schreiber was classmate William Meenagh. Meenagh's plane developed engine trouble and had to fall out of the formation. Pilot Hewitt ("Shorty") Wheless refused to turn back even though he knew he would have no protection from the machine guns of the other bombers on the mission. The crew proceeded to the Legaspi target area alone and arrived after the other craft had dropped their bombs and departed. In their dogged persistence, they had no idea that the news of their mission would stir a sensation all across America.

Lt Raymond Teborek, the copilot, related the story.

> We had planned on going over the target at 8,000 feet. On our climb-out to altitude, we had trouble keeping up with the others. We had turbo problems and a bad engine. We fell behind the rest of the flight and finally managed to get to 10,000 feet. Shorty decided that we continue on with the mission as he didn't think we would have any fighter interference and very little antiaircraft fire. We lost sight of the rest of the flight and proceeded on to the target area. As we approached Legaspi Bay, I could see six ships in the harbor. I guess they were troop transports but I didn't see them unloading personnel or material. About this time, we encountered flak and started our bomb run. About the same time as I saw the flak, I also saw six fighters coming up at us from one o'clock below. I alerted the crew about the fighters and they said, "Hell, they're coming from behind." All hell broke loose. To get away from the fighters and continue on the bomb run, Shorty went into a shallow dive. Our bombardier, Sergeant Schlotte, had one heck of a time trying to keep on target with our increase of A/S [airspeed] and change of altitude. The bombs were dropped in trail. Bill Meenagh and Sergeant Schlotte reported one hit and some near misses. We made only one run and didn't stick around for any confirmation. As those Zero's continued to work us over, I believe we were credited with sinking one transport. As soon as we dropped the bombs, Shorty broke off to the left into some sparse cloud coverage. The Zero's couldn't see us and were attacking from above.

Their incendiaries, explosive and armor piercing rounds came popping into the cockpit. One round went between and below two prop feathering switches. If one of the switches had been hit, we would have had an engine feathered with no way of getting it started again. Luck was on our side. Incendiaries hit the instrument panel. Shorty and I both received superficial burns on our legs. One explosive round hit the top of my armor plating and sprayed splinters of metal into my head. Shorty twisted and turned trying to stay in the clouds. I tried to see where the clouds were thick and told him where to turn. At one point I could see trees below and sloping terrain. We were coming upon a volcanic peak. I yelled at Shorty to swing left. Thank God that he did or we would have clobbered into that peak. We once again were in the clear and the Zeros made a few more passes at us and then left us alone. We concluded that the Zero's had used up all their ammo and therefore broke off the fight.

About ten minutes later, when we felt we were in the clear, Shorty asked me to check on the crew in the back. As I was going through the bomb bay, we hit a little turbulence and I grabbed for the control cables to steady myself. It was then that I found that most of our control cables had been severed, including the stabilizer control cable. Those cables that were holding were frayed and it was questionable if they would hold together. Checking on the crew, I found that Corporal Williams, who manned the top 50s in the radio compartment, had taken an explosive round in the thigh. I put a tourniquet on his leg and made him comfortable. Private Killin, our radio operator, was handling the belly guns—he had been shot in the head and was dead. Sergeant Gootee, crew chief, manned one of the waist guns and was wounded in the hand. Sgt R. D. Brown, the other waist gunner, literally had his winter flying jacket ripped to shreds—none of the rounds hit his flesh. The only crew members not injured were Lieutenant Meenagh and Sergeant Schlotte in the nose. I told Shorty the condition of our crew and about the control cables.

Shorty told Lieutenant Meenagh to plot a course back to Del Monte. We had to feather number one engine and another one was acting up. There was a big hole behind number three engine—it must of been some flak that hit us and ruptured the gas tank. Anyway, we had to transfer fuel from the left wing to the right wing to keep number three engine going. We encountered squall lines all the way back. We were able to maintain about 500 feet off the deck. At one point on our way back, going through a squall, the left wing went down because of turbulence. I was doing the driving. I gave right aileron and it continued to drop to the left. I gave more right and gradually the wing came up. Meenagh had his work cut out for him. With our dodging storms and darkness coming on, it made it difficult for him to navigate. Bill did an excellent job getting us to Cagayan. Being low on fuel, the rain and it getting dark, we had to get on the ground. We knew we couldn't climb high enough to get on the plateau at Del Monte, our base. We knew if we ditched in the bay at Cagayan we might not get our wounded out so our only other alternative was to try and land at the airfield at Cagayan which had a runway of about 2,000 feet long. We found the field but it had some carabao grazing in it. Shorty said, "Hell, it was now or never." We had Meenagh and Schlotte come upstairs, out of the nose and made sure our men were braced in the rear for a crash landing. We flew out over the water, dropped and checked our landing gear—all seemed okay. Knowing we couldn't trim the aircraft with the stabilized control when the flaps were lowered, Shorty said "Tebo, when I drop the flaps, you get on the controls with me and help me feel it in for a landing." (What I was doing was to compensate for our approach angle. The nose drops when you lower flaps and you have to roll the stabilizer control back to compensate.) As we dropped lower and got closer to the field, we could see tree trunks strewn about as barriers to prevent landing. Shoot, we were committed. We tripped off some tree tops near the end of the field, and hit the ground wheels first. It was then we knew our tires were flat. We bounced, hit again and we held her down—bounding over tree trunks like a bucking bronco. The rims dug in on the waterlogged field. We could feel our nose going down and I knew we were going to go up on our nose. We braced for the impact. The force was tremendous—although I had braced myself, I was forced forward and I used my hands to cushion my head as I hit the instrument panel. Shorty had the presence of mind to hit the master ignition switch to cut off all electrical power to prevent a fire. We went up on our nose and then very gently settled back to a perfect three point position. Meenagh released and pushed open the escape hatch and we all climbed out, slid down the wing and hit the ground on the double. Gas was pouring out of the wing and could have exploded. I waited a minute or two, and then with Shorty, Meenagh and Schlotte, I rushed back to help get the wounded out from the rear of the plane. It was only minutes later after we crash landed that we had help from the local people. We were driven to the local hospital for treatment. I had the splinters pulled out of my head. Sergeant Gootee and Corporal Williams were operated on and left in the hospital. The rest of us were driven to Del Monte by a Philippine army third lieutenant in a jeep, in pouring rain, driving with blackout lights on a narrow treacherous road. That ride from Cagayan to Del Monte was almost as harrowing as our mission. We got back to Del Monte around eleven o'clock. Pat MyIntyre, operations officer at the time, had just finished writing us off the books.[1]

The 19th Bombardment Group's big raid had been a fiasco by almost any measure. The proposed six-plane raid had turned out to be a three-plane raid with two of the three big B-17 bombers totally destroyed.

Dragged down by a succession of defeats, death, and destruction of aircraft, US morale was at a low ebb. At that time, President Franklin Roosevelt thrilled the nation by relating the story of the Shorty Wheless bomber crew who refused to think of defeat regardless of the odds against them. Radio and newspapers carried the story all around the world.

The ill-fated Legaspi mission was the last raid to be flown by planes based at Del Monte Field. Henceforth Del Monte would be used as a staging base for bombers flying from Australia and Java. Del Monte bombers were moved to Batchelor Field near Darwin, Australia. William Meenagh flew there three days later on 17 December 1941 with Shorty Wheless, Ray Teborek, and crew. Sergeant Gootee and Corporal Williams remained in the hospital at Cagayan. Other classmates who flew from the Philippines to Australia that day were Eddie Oliver, Arthur Hoffman, and Walter Seamon. George Markovick flew to Australia the following day.

So great was Captain Wheless' fame as a result of President Roosevelt's speech that the Air Corps sent the captain to the United States to star in a Warner Brothers' movie entitled, *Beyond the Line of Duty.* Meenagh and the remainder of the crew continued flying combat missions against the enemy.

At Batchelor Field, Colonel Eubank had the job of picking up the pieces and reorganizing the effort against the Japanese. Much had happened in the nine days since that first attack on Clark Field. Numerous raids had been conducted against enemy shipping and the Japanese landings on Luzon, but they had done little to slow the advance of the enemy. Twenty-one

Regroup

Six American Flying Fortresses flew south to Batchelor Field, Australia, on 17 December 1941. Though I (Ed Whitcomb) was working in communications at Clark Field handling all of the radio traffic, I was totally unaware of their departure or that it was the beginning of the end of our operations from air bases in the Philippine Islands. It had been less than two months since we had flown our beautiful, new, shiny Flying Fortresses from Australia to Clark Field ending the long trip from Albuquerque, New Mexico.

Citations to the crews of the flight read as follows:

> For meritorious achievement while participating in the first mass flight of B-17's from Albuquerque, New Mexico, to Clark Field, Pampanga, Luzon, P.I. as a member of a combat crew October-November, 1941. The flight of the 19th Bombardment Group (H) from the United States across the Pacific Ocean to the Philippine Islands was performed at the time when the successful accomplishment of the mission proved to have a direct bearing upon the security of the United States. Despite adverse weather, small airdromes, inadequate radio aids, and long over water flights with no alternate landing fields, the mission was accomplished within a short period of time. The performance of duty of each combat crew member resulted in the safe arrival of all airplanes involved on the flight.[1]

We had been a proud outfit and confident of an early victory over the Japanese if they were foolish enough to start a war against us. Ten days of war had shown us very clearly that we were facing a formidable enemy and that victory would not be easy. It seemed that everything that could go wrong had gone wrong for us and everything had gone right for the enemy. In two weeks time they had virtually destroyed US air and naval power in the Philippines.

The initial landings of Japanese ground forces at Aparri, Vigan, and Legaspi had been met by only token opposition by the Flying Fortresses. Then the 19th Bombardment Group started its move to Australia five days before the main Japanese invasion of the Philippines. When the move to Australia was completed, it turned out that Jack Jones, Jay Horowitz, William Warner, and I were the only navigators of our class left behind in the Philippines except George Berkowitz who was lying in a hospital in Manila with an amputated leg waiting for the Red Cross ship to transport him and 247 other casualties to Australia.

For those who flew to Batchelor Field in Australia, it did not take long for them to swing into action. Five days after their departure from the Philippines, four of the navigators, Anthony Oliver, Arthur Hoffman, William Meenagh, and Walter Seamon, were on a nine-plane mission from Australia back to the Philippines. They bombed Japanese warships in Davao Harbor and landed at Del Monte after dark. The following morning at 0315 four planes each loaded with seven 300-pound bombs took off to attack a huge convoy of warships in Lingayen Gulf. It turned out to be the main Japanese invasion fleet comprised of 43,110 men making its landing in the Philippines.* The four planes dropped their bombs in train but were unable to observe the results. They encountered antiaircraft fire and enemy aircraft but suffered no losses. That night they landed back at Ambon in the Dutch East Indies and returned to Batchelor Field the following day.

George ("Mark") Markovich was on a two-plane raid against the airport at Davao dropping bombs from 15,000 feet when his plane was hit by antiaircraft fire injuring two crew members. The two bombers climbed to 28,000 feet in an effort to evade a swarm of enemy fighters. Mark's bomber knocked one of the fighters out of the sky in the ensuing battle, but the crew reported that the Japanese fighters out-performed the Fortresses even at 28,000 feet.

The missions from Australia to the Philippines were grueling for the aircrews flying long hours at high altitudes and going without adequate rest for long periods of time. No aircrews in history had flown farther to deliver bombs on an enemy. They could not stop the landing of enemy troops in the Philippines

---

*The Japanese began landing their main invasion fleet of 43,000 men at Lingayen Gulf on 22 December 1941.

but there was a matter of greater concern. The Japanese were moving in the direction of the rich oil fields of Borneo. The planes of the 19th were moved from Batchelor Field to Malang, Java, in an effort to slow the enemy's southern movement. They would continue to bomb targets in the Philippines from Java.*

Java offered a respite for the war-weary flyers. Far from the mud and mosquitoes of the Philippine jungles, they were quartered in the Palace Hotel and brick barracks where they could enjoy good food and drink of their choice. There were two large hangars for maintenance and repairs of their aircraft. Things were looking up. For months the flyers had heard that help was on the way and for the first time they had reason to believe it. The 7th Bombardment Group from Salt Lake City had been scheduled to join them in the Philippines with fresh crews and new airplanes. With them would be four more navigation classmates including Richard Cease, George Walthers, Robert Trenkle, and Paul Dawson. In addition there had been a persistent rumor that a big convoy was headed for the Philippines including seven transports loaded with a wealth of reinforcements. It carried the ground elements of the 7th Bombardment Group together with 18 P-40s, 52 A-24 dive bombers, 500,000 rounds of .50 caliber armor-piercing and tracer ammunition, 9,600 rounds of high explosive for 37-mm antiaircraft guns, 2,000 500-pound bombs, and miscellaneous vehicles and equipment together with 4,600 troops. It seemed logical that since it contained the ground elements of the 7th Bombardment Group, it should come to Java. The authorities had explored every possible avenue for getting the convoy to the Philippines to support General MacArthur. Gen Dwight D. Eisenhower, at the time serving as chief of staff, Third Army at Fort Sam Houston, Texas, was selected by Gen George C. Marshall to work out a solution to the problem.[2]

In the meantime the aircrews, with hardly time to get acquainted with their new environment, were off on another mission to Davao in the Philippines. It appeared that the harbor there was a staging area for Japanese ships on their way to Borneo. Oliver and Seamon flew with nine Fortresses to

---

*The 19th Bombardment Group deployed to Java in late January 1942.

Davao on 3 January 1942. They staged through Samarinda, Borneo, and flew the 730 nautical miles to find the harbor crowded with one battleship, five cruisers, six destroyers, 12 submarines, and numerous small craft. Going in at 25,000 feet they observed antiaircraft fire up to their altitude but behind their planes. Fighters were unable to close on them because of their altitude. All planes returned safely to Malang.

Notes

1. War Department General Order 14, 19 February 1944.
2. Entrusted by Army chief of staff Gen George Marshall with $10 million in gold and cash for the purpose of aiding MacArthur and his beleaguered forces, Eisenhower sought to hire ships and crews willing to attempt running the Japanese blockade of the Philippines. Unfortunately, in early 1942 precious few mariners were willing to risk that trip for any price. This episode is briefly recounted in Geoffrey Perret, *Winged Victory: The Army Air Forces in World War II* (New York: Random House, 1993), 149.

Richard Wellington Cease

The 19th Bombardment Group started withdrawing from the Philippines nine days after the attack on Clark Field. Group headquarters was established at Batchelor Field near Port Darwin, Australia. After the Legaspi mission, all bombing raids against the Japanese in the Philippines were conducted by planes based in Australia or Java. From that time on, missions to the Philippines were staged through Del Monte Field. The bomber would leave Australia or Java and plan to arrive at Del Monte Field at dusk and depart before dawn to avoid being strafed by Japanese fighters. With only five hours of rest at Del Monte, some of the crews flew as long as 25 hours on the 30-hour Philippine missions. Targets for such raids were the troop landings on the island of Luzon and shipping in the important Davao Bay on the southeast coast of the island of Mindanao.

In the meantime, a large contingent of flyers and ground crews were stranded at Del Monte from January until the surrender of the Philippines in May. A number of them were able to get to Australia on bombers returning from missions elsewhere in the Philippines. Others were captured and spent the remainder of the war in prison camps. Classmates who were able to get to Australia from Del Monte included Walter Seamon, John Cox, Jr., Charles Stevens, Anthony Oliver, Arthur Hoffman, Harry Schreiber, George Markovich, Harold McAuliff, and William Meenagh.

In late December 1941, most of the bombers moved from Australia to Java where they continued their raids against the Philippines and Borneo. No new planes or supplies had reached the Philippines. Aircrews were weary from the long hard missions and morale was at a very low ebb.

In Java, word came that the long-awaited new planes with fresh crews would be arriving from the United States. There was new hope. Until reinforcement planes arrived, the 19th Group had only C and D models of the B-17. These had no tail guns and had only a single .30-caliber machine gun in the plexiglass nose of each plane for defense against frontal attacks. The light machine gun seemed more like a toy than a weapon to defend the big bombers. There were a number of holes in the plexiglass nose, and the navigator or bombardier had the job of getting the gun into the right position to fire on an approaching plane. The good news was that the new planes had twin .50-caliber machine guns in the tail. With sufficient planes, the aircrews felt that they could stop the Japanese and turn the tide of the war. Classmates arriving in Java with the new equipment included George Walthers, Paul Dawson, Robert Trenkle, and Richard Cease.

Cease was a serious-minded young man from the back mountain country of Pennsylvania where his father had long been a manual training teacher. Being one of the first boys from his community to go into combat, Cease received considerable notoriety. Dr G. L. Howell, a local physician, had been asked by the press if he knew Richard. "Did I know Dick? I brought him into the world. He played with my boy and peddled the (Wilkes-Barre) *Record* all around these hills. When he was about fourteen he used to milk Josephine Hazeltine's cows and help her with the chores every day. He was one of the best boys in this town."[1] In that statement, Dr Howell expressed the sentiments of all Kingston Township citizens according to the local newspaper.

Richard Cease arrived in Malang, Java, on 18 January 1942 bringing the number of new planes from the States to 10 B-17Es and five LB-30s. Excerpts from his letters home tell of his hopes and aspirations, dreams, patriotic spirit, and love for country.

Ft Douglas, Utah
24 November 1941

Dear Folks,

You said in your letter that you had received my letter containing the will and the Power of Attorney. Don't feel bad about the will, everybody should have a will because it makes things easier if something does happen. . . . And let me know if you get your allotment. It is supposed to start this month and the check will be mailed direct to you. Do anything you like and bank the rest. When I get back I would like to have a little bank balance—maybe to get married who knows? How was your Thanksgiving at home? Was it a happy day? I had my dinner at Anne's and it was mighty fine. We went to the game and had dinner. Yes, she is the same girl as the picture I had at home. Her last name is Wright, and she is from a mighty fine family.[2]

Ft Douglas, Utah
30 November 1941

Dear Folks,

I received your letter yesterday and was very glad to get it. I liked everything but the note of worry in it, Mother. It is easy for me to say please do not worry for I know that you probably can't. But try to look at the brighter side of things and there are many things for which we should be thankful.

Ft Douglas, Utah
5 December 1941

Dear Folks,

I wish that I could save a little in the time to come so that when I get back we could get married. I'm not sure but I think she would. You would like her Mother and I hope that you can meet her sometime. But time changes things and we may not be able to tell just what will happen. When you receive this we may be on our way—don't worry for it isn't as bad as it seems. We are going to have a wonderful trip and I'll tell you all about it when we get there.

Mirror Lake [California]
10 December 1941

Dear Folks,

We as Americans now have a job to do and, that is to retain what we have, and that is to whip those bandits. We have just got to avenge for that deal in Hawaii. The people will just have to take things seriously and do as the President said, share the good and bad news alike. This is a season of the year when love should reign in our hearts and I'm sure that in the hearts of Americans it does, but I'm sure that we have a job to do in preserving this nation and the world so that love can prevail. It is going to cost us, sure, heart sickness, worry, loss of lives and money, but we must do it. So lets resign ourselves to what may come, what do you say, huh? We are a God loving nation so what do we have to worry about?

Hamilton Field, California
27 December 1941

Dear Folks,

Well Mother I am glad that you have decided the way that you have. Now I'll know that when I go you won't worry about me. There are millions of us going to go and I'll be just one of them.

Grande Hotel
Belém-Para-Brazil
6 January 1941 [sic 1942]

Dear Folks,

Everything is fine but by the time we get to our destination we will be tired out but we must keep right on going if we are ever to get there. How is everything in the States? You will never know how much you could miss a place so much. Don't ever let anybody take the United States from you. I can see that anything that is good, the US has it. You can only imagine the conditions you see in some of these countries.

American Forces in Palace Hotel, Java
29 January 1942

Dear Folks,

Well as you can see I am here in (censored) Java. Java as you know is one of the East Indies. First of all, how is everybody at home? Did you by any chance receive any of the packages I sent? I hope that you like the candlesticks, Mother. There is quite a story behind them that I will tell you when I get home and I hope that is soon.

Those great United States, the trouble is we don't appreciate them enough. One never realizes what they are and what they have to offer until he gets out and sees the world.

It had become necessary for the new planes to fly east to the Philippines instead of across the Pacific as in the earlier flights. Japanese advances made the Pacific route untenable. Navigators went to the US Hydrographic Office in Washington, D.C., and selected maps suitable for the long route from the US to the Philippines via South America, Africa, and Asia. They then navigated on routes never flown before. Meteorological data, radio facilities, and support for such a trip were woefully inadequate and even nonexistent in some stops along the way. With all of their planning and preparations, not one of the planes reached the Philippines, but instead found their way to Australia and Java.

Everyone knew that there was a rush to get planes to the Far East, but few realized how desperate the situation had become. Colonel Eubank reported that the United States Air Corps, at the forefront of World War II in the Pacific, had but eight B-17 bombers in flying condition for high-altitude missions. That was their strength on the first day of 1942. In the days that followed, he sent mission after mission of six, seven, or eight of his big bombers against the Japanese. The bombers attacked ships in Davao Harbor in the Philippines, 730 nautical miles from the bases in Java. They also attacked Japanese warships along the coast of Borneo and in the Makassar Strait. In Java a very small band of valiant aircrews sought to hold things together until reinforcements could arrive from the States via the African route. Bravery and gallantry in action were the orders of the day, with crews flying high-altitude missions day after day without fighter escort. They were trying desperately to fend off the fast, high-flying Zero fighters. Later when I asked navigator Walter E. Seamon how many missions he had flown in Java, he admitted that he did not know. He was off one plane and into another. Like other navigators, he kept no log book. They wrote information for the missions on their maps and then erased it before the next mission.

Richard W. Cease arrived in Malang on 18 January 1942. He learned that aircrews were sighting more and more Japanese warships as the days went by. The enemy was moving into the rich oil fields of Borneo and also through the Makassar Strait toward Java.

On January 22d, just four days after his arrival from the grueling flight from the US, Cease flew his first combat mission. He was navigating for Maj Stanley K. Robinson, commander of the 7th Bombardment Group. Two days later he flew on another mission that sank one transport and shot down five enemy aircraft. The new B-17E planes with their tail guns surprised the Japanese fighter pilots, and US gunners had a field day blasting Zeros out of the sky.

On 26 January, Cease's mission to Balikpapan, Borneo, turned back on account of weather. His mission the next day resulted in reports of one transport sunk and four fighters shot out of the skies. On 29 January the target was warships in the Makassar Strait. Thirty Zero fighters attacked his plane on the second pass over the target. Harold McAuliff, a classmate who was navigating another plane on the same mission, reported, "We were bombing the Japanese fleet in the Makassar Strait and getting shot up by flack and Zeros. As the attack broke off and we headed for home, Robinson's airplane went into a long dive and just kept on going until it hit the water. There was no fire and the only thing we could figure out was that the controls were shot out or the pilots were dead or badly wounded." The plane carried a crew of nine flyers including Richard Cease to their watery graves.

There in the vast reaches of the Makassar Strait off the coast of Borneo, circular waves rolled out from the point of impact apparently as peacefully as from a pebble dropped into a quiet brook. It was unreal as a silent movie as the awe-stricken airmen in the five other planes looked on. With those waves went all of the hopes and dreams of a serious-minded young man from the back mountain country of Pennsylvania. He had dreamed of saving some money and coming back to the land he loved so dearly to marry Anne Wright, but all of those dreams vanished just as the waves vanished as the sea became calm again.

Notes

1. *The Dallas Post*, Dallas, Pennsylvania, Friday, 20 February 1942.
2. Letters provided by Philip Cease, brother of Richard Cease, 1990.

Paul E. Dawson

During the two-week period after Richard Cease died, B-17 aircrews suffered tremendous losses. Crews and planes were being lost almost as rapidly as new planes were arriving from the States. Nine B-17s on a mission to bomb the Japanese-held Dutch base of Kendari were seriously mauled by Japanese fighters. Classmate Paul E. Dawson related the story:

> I well remember the mission when Capt Dufrane was leading the flight at 7,000 feet. We were on our way from our base at Malang, Java. At about 180 miles off Bali cloud cover was solid beneath us when we inadvertently flew over a Japanese aircraft carrier and its escort. Shortly thereafter we had fighters all over us. Dufrane got the worst of it because the Japanese believed that the lead plane was the only one with a bombsight.

> After Dufrane's plane was hit and going down, our plane was coming up to lead the formation. I saw his plane turret gunner bail out right in front of my eyes. He was a big fellow and could not wear his parachute while manning the gun in his position; so he kept it on the floor. When the plane was hit, he did not have time to put the chute on properly and had hooked only the chest straps. Needless to say, when he pulled the rip cord without the leg straps latched, his arms flew skyward. The last time I saw him was when he was covering his eyes with his arms and falling into the sea. The entire crew bailed out over the sea and there was no chance to rescue any of them.

> The Japanese pilots would sometimes machine gun crew members who bailed out. To protect myself against that I used to carry a stopwatch and keep one eye on the altimeter so in case I had to bail out I could free fall and open the chute in the last few seconds of the fall.

> After Dufrane went down, our ship with Don Struthers as pilot took lead of the formation. Then the Japanese concentrated their fire on us. A 20-mm cannon shell hit our oxygen tank knocking out our hydraulic system, our brakes, landing gear and bomb release mechanism. We kicked the bombs out manually over Bali and returned to Java landing at Djokjakarta. Struthers crash-landed the plane wheels up with

no injuries to the crew. From there we had to hitchhike our way back to our base at Malang.

Three new planes were on the way from the States to Malang; so we divided our crew members up three ways. The young navigator told me I had selected the wrong plane because the pilot was a nut. When we arrived at Malang, I could see that he was right. We came in over the field too high and too fast. I remarked that he was not going to land on this strip. We crashed over a revetment and into a barbed wire entanglement wiping out the landing gear. I opened the bottom hatch and ran in case the plane caught fire. The pilot's only comment was, "Well, I brought you a nice mess of spare parts." They gave him a ground job on the spot.[1]

Thus Paul Dawson narrowly escaped death when a cannon shell hit his plane, survived a crash landing, and then a second crash landing all in one day. But that was not all. Dawson continued to fly mission after mission; then there was to be another crash landing.

It happened in the bush country of the York Peninsula on the northeastern tip of Australia. I had left Port Moresby on the 4th of July night to bomb Lae and Salamoa, New Guinea. (That is where Amelia Earhart took off when she disappeared on the way to Howland Island.) On returning to Port Moresby after the mission, the weather was so bad that I could not see the airport even though they had all of searchlights shining upwards. We decided to fly to Mitchell River Mission air strip on the York Peninsula, Australia. It was a grass strip only 300 meters long; but that was the closest place with clear weather. Even though the pilot had throttled back to economy cruising, we were so low on gas that we finally made a crash landing in the bush. I radioed our position but it was several days before an Australian flying boat, like we used for training at Coral Gables, came over us. It dropped some tea and a five gallon can of water. The tea was okay, but the water can burst when it hit the ground. We took water from the river to make our tea.

After about a week some aborigines came to us with some horses. They agreed to take us to the Mitchell River Mission; but the bush was so dense that it took us 24 hours to travel the five to ten miles to the mission. We were flown from there to a larger airstrip in a small plane; then a larger plane took us back to our base at Port Moresby.

The plucky Paul Dawson may have set some kind of record in surviving three crash landings. At war's end he left the military service and enjoyed a successful career as a professional deep-sea diver in the Caribbean Sea.

Notes

1. Paul E. Dawson to author, letter, subject: Kendari Mission, 1994.

George Markovich

Eleven March 1942 saw a bewildered and weary Gen Douglas MacArthur together with his wife, Jean, his five-year-old son, Arthur, Arthur's Chinese nurse, and a staff of 15 officers fleeing from the beleaguered island of Corregidor. He was leaving behind an army of 80,000 men including 12,000 Americans. More than that, he was leaving behind all of the plans, the preparations, and the equipment he had amassed for the purpose of defending the Philippine Islands against a Japanese invasion. It had taken a well-trained and highly-disciplined Japanese army just four months to run rough-shod over all of Field Marshal MacArthur's defenses. Defenses he had built up over the past six years.

MacArthur was not new to the Philippines. His father, Gen Arthur MacArthur, had led the American forces that defeated Filipino insurgents and captured Manila to mark the start of the American occupation of the islands in 1899.[1] Then just five years later as a young 2d lieutenant freshly commissioned from the United States Military Academy at West Point, Douglas MacArthur had been assigned to the Philippines on his first tour of active duty. Ironically, one of his first responsibilities had been to conduct an engineering survey of the peninsula of Bataan to develop a plan later refined and identified in April 1941 as War Plan Orange III (WPO III). The plan had been carried out, but as of March 1942 the flaw in the plan was glaringly apparent. The 80,000 soldiers who had been withdrawn to Bataan were bottled up. They could not get away, and reinforcements could not be delivered to them.

We had been there more than two months—fighting, starving, diseased and weary—when we learned that our commander was abandoning us and departing for Australia. Less than two months later, we would surrender to a savage and ruthless enemy, and we would suffer more cruel treatment than anyone could have imagined.

General MacArthur had doggedly persisted in his demands for more and more support from the national administration. He had been surprisingly successful. MacArthur did get the lion's share of heavy bombardment units in the Pacific before World War II started. Even though a report to Gen Hap Arnold, chief of the US Air Corps, had recommended that a minimum of 36 B-17 bombers would be necessary to defend Hawaii, ironically, on the day Pearl Harbor was attacked MacArthur had 35 B-17s in the Philippines while there were only 12 based in Hawaii.

In mid-March we flyers on Bataan learned that General MacArthur had left the Philippines and moved to Australia. His departure from the Philippines was, of course, ordered by Commander in Chief Franklin Delano Roosevelt. So brilliant an officer could not be sacrificed at a time when America faced monumental military problems; however, the general's brilliance had not shown through in the early stages of the war. Air Corps planes which should have been unleashed against the invading enemy forces were annihilated on the ground nine hours after the Japanese had attacked Pearl Harbor. Additionally, the Japanese landing forces had not been repulsed in their major landings on the island. Blunders were rife and military writers since that time have not hesitated to lay the blame squarely at the doorstep of Gen Douglas MacArthur.[2]

US Navy commander John Bulkely picked up the general and his party at the South Mine Dock of Corregidor at 2000 hours on Wednesday, 12 March 1942. After hours of dodging Japanese naval craft, their PT boats traversed the 560 water miles to the city of Cagayan on the island of Mindinao near the Del Monte Air Field. It was a very difficult trip and the general and all members of his family were ill from the roughness of the sea.

Flying Fortresses that were supposed to be waiting for the general at Del Monte Field were nowhere to be seen. The war had been going so badly that the 19th Bombardment Group was hard-pressed to provide transportation for the general.

After three impatient days, a restless general and his party crowded onto a war-weary B-17 and flew to Port Darwin, Australia. The general had good reason to be concerned about his safety and the safety of his party. The long flight from Del Monte Field to Australia was over enemy-held territory where the Japanese had the capability of shooting his plane out of the sky. It was an uncomfortable but uneventful trip to Australia. Just one year later, Japanese Admiral Yamamoto was ambushed and shot down in flames by American P-38 fighter planes on just such a long, over-water flight. Yamamoto had been the architect of the Japanese attack on Pearl Harbor and was Japan's greatest hero at the time he was shot down on 18 April 1943.

Upon General MacArthur's arrival safe and secure in Port Darwin, Australia, he made it clear that he wanted nothing more to do with airplanes. Since there were no trains from Port Darwin, he was determined to travel by automobile. It was 1,000 miles across the northern Australian bush country to the nearest railroad. His doctor advised him that due to his little son's illness, he should travel by air. He then relented and agreed to fly to Alice Springs where he could catch a train to Melborne. His staff, traveling by air, reached Melborne several days ahead of the general.

In Australia, great crowds were waiting to greet General MacArthur. An aura of greatness surrounded the defeated general. So great was his popularity that each morning crowds of people waited across the street from his hotel just to see him enter his staff car for his trip to headquarters.

The Australian government quickly placed its military forces under his command, and he was soon elevated to the position of supreme commander of the Allied Forces in the Southwest Pacific.

His headquarters at Melborne was far removed from the American forces fighting in New Guinea. Thus it became apparent that air travel was to become a fact of life for the general, much as he detested it. He would have his own personal plane with a crew assigned to him.

Until the time they were chosen as crew members for the general's personal plane, these flyers had been fighting a losing war in the southwest Pacific. Henry ("Hank") Godman had been pilot on one of four planes originally ordered to rescue the MacArthur party from the Philippines. Disaster had struck as he was approaching the field at night. He had crashed at sea. Two of his crew members had died, but Hank had been able to swim to shore.

In Australia, Henry Godman was selected to be the pilot for General MacArthur's first airplane. Then it became Godman's duty to select the best crew he could find for the plane. On one of his earlier bombing missions, he had been impressed by his navigator, Capt George M. ("Mark") Markovich. He knew that, in addition to being a brilliant navigator, Markovich held a bachelor of arts degree from the University of California at Berkeley and that he spoke seven different languages. Also, he knew that Markovich was a member of the Class of 40-A who had navigated across the Pacific and gone through the Philippine Campaign with the 19th Bombardment Group.

George Markovich had been in the hospital with malaria fever when the 19th Bombardment Group had returned to the United States after its Philippine and Java campaigns. Though he was eligible to return to the States, he was glad to stay on as a member of the general's crew. From that time, his life took a different turn. Working for the general was like working for royalty.

One of the crew's first assignments was to return to Wright-Patterson Field, Ohio, to take delivery of a new B-17 Flying Fortress. It had been fashioned especially for General MacArthur. That trip gave Markovich his first opportunity since he had left home many months before to visit his mother and father in Long Beach.

At home Mark was greeted with open arms. There was great happiness that Mark had returned home safely; yet there was also sadness. Mark explained,

> I remember the tears and sorrow of a family that was close friends of our family. When I returned home, the woman could not understand why I was still alive and her son shot down over Germany. Why? I recalled the words of my Father just prior to our departure for P.I. He knew that the US was going to be involved in the war, and both he and Mom wanted me to come back. He went on to say that should I lose my life in the war, they would be proud that their son made the supreme sacrifice for his country. My Dad said: "This country is worth fighting for."[3]

The words of the Serbian immigrant had instilled a strong spirit of Americanism in his son. It was that spirit that kept George Markovich in the Pacific war long after he was eligible for return to the United States.

At Wright-Patterson Field, upon instructions from the general, a map of the Philippines was painted across the nose of the shiny new airplane. Over that was printed the word "Bataan." As Pilot Godman described it:

> They painted a beautiful picture in oils on the right and left side of the nose of that B-17. They were really proud of their work and the fact that they had worked on General MacArthur's airplane. . . . The bombay tanks and braces had been taken out; and in their place were two Pullman bunks, an electric stove and an icebox. The radio compartment had been converted into a sitting room furnished beautifully with a desk, chairs and all. The interior of the plane was absolutely beautiful.[4]

After the final touches had been put on the plane at Wright-Patterson Field, the prize aircraft had to be flown to Washington, D.C., for inspection by Gen Henry ("Hap") Arnold. The red carpet of warm hospitality was rolled out at every stop when the *Bataan* was in the traffic pattern. The aura of General MacArthur's greatness was with it.

Then came the long, long flight from Washington, D.C., back to Australia. There the sight of the *Bataan* brought a new hope and new enthusiasm to the American and Australian forces.

In Australia, Markovich found that the Australian people greeted American servicemen with warm hospitality. Even in Sydney, far away from the shooting war, the people supported Americans in every way. Together the Americans and Australians had stopped the invading Japanese before the enemy had reached the mainland. The Australians were grateful.

When he was flying missions in the Philippines and in Java, Markovich could never have dreamed of the life that awaited him in Sydney. There he was housed in a general's apartment on the beach and assigned a Dodge staff car. The car was not in a good state of repair but it provided transportation. In his spare time, he found an abundance of female companionship was available at his beck and call.

Markovich was enjoying his new life to the fullest until Hank Godman issued him a challenge. "Mark, I don't think you know a decent girl."

Mark thought about that for a moment. He knew exactly what Hank meant, but he countered with, "What do you mean by that?"

He knew that Hank was a married man and that he did not approve of the type of company Mark was keeping.

"I mean just what I said. I'll bet you ten pounds [$33.00] that you do not know a decent girl," Hank replied.

Markovich was deep in thought. He remembered a pretty girl by the name of June, the daughter of Dr F. Justin McCarthy. She drove a vehicle for the United Service Organizations (USO) in Sydney. On occasion she had given him a lift when his old Dodge had refused to run. The only problem with her was that she had a reputation for not liking Yanks. She would not go out with them.

"Yes, I do know a decent girl," was Mark's feeble reply.

A few weeks later Mark saw June again. He described it:

> One day as I left HQ building I heard this feminine voice calling me. My first thought was that the protocol sergeant had ordered me a staff car. I thought I should go tell the poor girl that I had my own transportation. As I leaned into the window of the car, it was June! We talked a while and then I left. My first thought was that perhaps she did not mind Yanks after all. A week later I tried to get a date with her, no luck. I tried this a number of times until finally she said that if I would call a week in advance that perhaps she would accept my invitation to dinner. I finally made a date with June and we met Hank for a drink and small talk before dinner. As we left, Hank stuck the 10 pound note in my hand.[5]

Markovich navigated the general from Brisbane to the war zone about once each month. Then on the morning of 25 February 1944, Hank Godman greeted Markovich with, "Mark, you'd better start packing your bags."

When Mark inquired about where they were going, the reply was, "Back to the exotic south sea island known as New Guinea."

They spent the morning checking the *Bataan* and departed with the general aboard for the five-hour flight to the forward headquarters. It was an easy flight. Markovich was able to maintain his course and determine his ground speed by use of the drift meter on a "double drift" procedure.

On the ground, the general was driven to what the GI's referred to as the "Palace." That evening Markovich and Godman were invited to join the general for dinner before retiring for the night.

Markovich recalls about the general:

> On the eve of the landing in the Admiralty Islands he was, at one o'clock in the morning, prancing up and down the screened-in porch just in front of my room. Thinking that he might be sick, I jumped out of bed and approached him and asked if he was all right. He said "Yes." Then he went on to say that in the morning we would hit the islands, but what bothered him most was the thought of losing even one American. Markovich, being close to the general, developed a deep appreciation for his compassion and for his concerns.[6]

MacArthur departed early in the morning for Milne Bay where he boarded the USS *Phoenix*, his flagship during the Admiralty operation. The strategy for the landing had been nearly perfect and the general seemed pleased. He was in excellent spirits when he boarded the *Bataan* for the flight back to Brisbane.

When they were not flying, Markovich and Godman acted as aides for their boss, running errands, maintaining the map of the battle area on the wall and taking care of various problems. At the general's request, they did not salute upon entering or departing from his office.

Markovich recalled that at one meeting in the general's conference room,

> Nimitz, Kinkaid, Shappard (USMC), Kenney, Southerland, and other military specialists met to discuss the tactics for driving the Japanese forces from the New Guinea area. The Navy wanted to take 20,000 Marines and 25,000 sailors to hit Raboul. The general did not agree. A rather lively discussion resulted. It finally terminated when the general pounded the table and said, "Gentlemen, I am the supreme commander of the South Pacific."

> Months later I learned what this man was all about when we flew him up to the headquarters in New Guinea. Hank and I were always invited to have dinner with the general. After dinner he would get his cigar and a glass of port or something like that. He would say to us, "You gentlemen may smoke it if you wish." It was here that I was able to talk to him. I used to marvel at the ability and intelligence of this rather superior man. We would get into a lively conversation about a lot of things. I once asked him to compare the tactics of this war with the principles of Clausewitz. His answer was that with Clausewitz [ian] tactics you couldn't fight an enemy who conducted themselves like animals, you must practically lower yourself to the level of the beast.[7]

The general was frustrated by the Japanese tactics in jungle warfare, procedures not taught to US military personnel at that time.

When Hank Godman left General MacArthur's crew and went back to flying combat, Markovich made a request to go with him. Then the general intervened. "Didn't you just get married?" he asked Markovich.

When Markovich acknowledged the fact, the general said, "I think that you owe her more than the worries she would have if you went back to combat."

That settled the matter. George Markovich had been in the Pacific Theater to see his air group driven out of the Philippines and Java. He had navigated Gen Douglas MacArthur on the 5,000 mile trip back to Hawaii for his historic meeting with President Roosevelt. There he saw him designated the supreme allied commander in the Southwest Pacific. When Markovich departed for home, the Yanks were on the move. They were on the long road that would see them once again back in the Philippines and on to Japan.

He had come to know General MacArthur intimately. He respected and admired him deeply. The navigator had attended meetings with all of the great leaders in the South Pacific war. He was ready to go home. But he had another good reason for wanting to go home. He had married a pretty Australian girl by the name of June McCarthy. He wanted to show her to his parents, and he wanted to show her America.

Notes

1. A hero and literal "boy colonel" (at age 19) in the Civil War, Arthur MacArthur went to the Philippines in July 1898 as a brigadier general. A successful field commander in the bloody and protracted struggle with Filipino nationalists known as the Philippine Insurrection (1899–1902), the elder MacArthur was promoted to major general in 1899 and named military governor of the Philippines the following year. In 1901 he was removed from that position for insubordination to William Taft, president of the US Philippine Commission and later governor of the Philippines. Bitter at being passed over for Army chief of staff, Arthur MacArthur, by then a lieutenant general, resigned his commission in 1909. Arthur MacArthur's colorful career is summarized in William Manchester, *American Caesar: Douglas MacArthur, 1880–1964* (Boston: Little, Brown and Co., 1978), 13–38. See also D. Clayton James, *The Years of MacArthur*, vol. 1 (Boston: Houghton Mifflin, 1970–1985); and Carol M. Petillo, *Douglas MacArthur: The Philippine Years* (Bloomington, Ind.: Indiana University Press, 1981).

2. For a recent and critical appraisal of MacArthur's role in the Philippine debacle see Ronald H. Spector, *Eagle Against the Sun: The American War with Japan* (New York: Free Press, 1985), xiv–xv, 106–19. Foremost among the many biographies of MacArthur is James. A fascinating psychological assessment is available in Petillo. Both James and Petillo offer candid and by no means always flattering appraisals of MacArthur's character and judgment. Most of the accounts written by former members of MacArthur's staff are adulatory in the extreme. An exception is the rich and insightful Jay Luvaas, ed., *Dear Miss Em: General Eichelberger's War in the Pacific, 1942–1945* (Westport, Conn.: Greenwood Press, 1972). Lt Gen Robert L. Eichelberger was one of MacArthur's leading ground commanders in the Pacific War.

3. George Markovich to author, letter, subject: Return Home, 1982.

4. Col Henry C. Godman and Cliff Dudley, *Supreme Commander* (Harrison, Ark.: New Leaf Press, 1980), 52.

5. George Markovich to author, letter, subject: WWII Experience, undated.

6. Ibid.

7. Ibid.

War Plan Orange III

Three of my classmates whose planes had been destroyed on the ground remained with me (Ed Whitcomb) at Clark Field when the 19th Group departed for Del Monte Field on Mindanao. With me were Jay Horowitz, William Warner, and Jack Jones. Since we did not have planes to navigate, we assumed other positions. I took a job in the communications section, encoding and decoding radio messages at the mobile radio station. Members of the communications section ate from a field kitchen which had been set up under the trees. Because I was on duty 24 hours a day, I slept on the ground outside the radio trailer. We endured air raids day after day, with the Japanese bombers coming over so low at times that we could see into the bomb bays as their bombs fell about us. The bombers were virtually unopposed, since we had no fighter planes at Clark Field.

Even though I was working in the communications section, I was unaware that the 19th Bombardment Group had evacuated Del Monte Field and moved to Batchelor Field, Australia, on 17 December 1941, only nine days after the first attack on Clark Field.

I was training to encode and decode messages. It seemed strange to me that there was not someone there who was already trained for such duty until I learned that the regular cryptographers had been moved to Corregidor or to bomb group headquarters.

There were code books which were very simple to use; but I suspected that the Japanese had the same books and were much handier with them than I. Then there was a set of disks about the size of checkers. On the outside of each disk were letters of the alphabet. The disks rotated on a spindle. It was like a puzzle. My job was to take the letters of the alphabet that came in on the radio and rotate the disks until all of the letters from the radio were in a row. Then I would rotate the thing until I could make out a sentence that made sense. The trouble with that was that the sender was using code words that were only understandable to the officer to whom I delivered the message.

On 24 December, the staff in the communications section packed equipment and prepared for a move. We had no idea of our destination; however, we were all glad to be leaving Clark Field, where we had been pounded so mercilessly by enemy bombers.

Shortly after noon, we found ourselves to be a part of an unbelievable convoy made up of every kind of military vehicle. At first, we headed toward Manila, about 56 miles to the south; but when we reached the city of San Fernando, we turned westward. The convoy moved slowly, with long delays from time to time. The farther we traveled, the more disabled vehicles we saw along the side of the road. The numbers grew into dozens, then hundreds, of abandoned vehicles of every description. Instead of an orderly withdrawal, it appeared to be more of a rout. If anything went wrong with a vehicle, it was abandoned. There was not time, or even inclination, to repair anything that was out of order.

Although we had traveled only about 70 miles, it was well after dark when we pulled off the main road. Then we followed a trail about one-quarter of a mile before we stopped for the night. It had been an unceremonious Christmas Eve for us confused and weary travelers.

On Christmas Day 1941, we arose and looked out across the waters of Manila Bay to the isle of Corregidor, to the south of us. In the distance to the southeast, we could see the radio towers of the Cavite Naval Base; to the east, we could make out a part of the skyline of Manila. We were on the peninsula of Bataan, just to the north of a coastal village by the name of Cabcaben.

Though we had no way of knowing it, this was the refuge provided for us under War Plan Orange III (WPO III). The plan had been worked out over past years, and it was said that it was well known to all US Army officers who had been in the Philippines six months or more. But I had been there less than two months. I knew nothing of it.[1]

We were there even though it had been well established by competent authority that the Philippine Islands could not be

72

defended by the United States in the event of war with Japan. As late as 1937, just four years before the outbreak of World War II, Gen Stanley D. Embick, then chief of the War Plans Division of the US Army, believed that in case of war with Japan, the United States should withdraw behind its natural strategic peacetime frontier in the Pacific—the line of Alaska, Oahu, and the Panama Canal. He knew the territory well. As a colonel on the General Staff after World War I, he had opposed the 1924 Orange Plan. Later, as commander of the army garrison on Corregidor, he had written a critique labelling "Orange" an "act of madness." Those of us who became victims of War Plan Orange III would wholeheartedly agree with Colonel Embick. The planners certainly never envisioned a situation where 80,000 troops would endeavor to fight a war with no reinforcements whatsoever against a Japanese army of 200,000 soldiers who were being regularly reinforced with fresh troops and supplies.[2]

Gen Leonard Wood, a former chief of staff of the US Army and later governor-general of the Philippines, had said that war with Japan would require "the abandonment of American posts, American soldiers, an American fleet, and American citizens in the Far East."[3] General Wood was right—that is exactly what happened!

Within three months after the outbreak of the war in the Pacific, all of the American military posts in the Philippines had been abandoned except the tiny island of Corregidor and some forces on Mindanao. The naval station at Subic Bay, Cavite Naval Base, Fort McKinley, Clark Field, Nichols Field, and Nielson Field lay in ruins and in the hands of the Japanese. Part of the American Pacific Fleet had been unable to escape from the islands, and had been captured or sent to the bottom of the sea; and 3,000 American citizens were languishing in Japanese internment camps at Santo Thomas University in Manila or at Baguio, 200 miles to the north. Almost every prediction by Gen Leonard Wood had come true!

Those troops who survived the first three months of the war had retreated to the peninsula of Bataan and the mighty fortress of Corregidor Island, protecting Manila Bay as contemplated under War Plan Orange III.

Medical supplies were depleted so that less than minimal care was available for the sick and wounded. Sick and wounded patients in the hospitals were spread out across the jungle, many without any shelter whatsoever.

The southern end of the Bataan peninsula was a beautiful place with tall mahogany trees and cool mountain streams, but the beauty was meaningless to us. We wanted so much to believe that reinforcements were on the way that we actually believed it would happen. We never gave up hope.

I set up a radio in the center of our camp area under four towering mango trees so that we could hear the shortwave newscasts from station KGEI San Francisco, 7,000 miles away. Evening after evening we heard President Roosevelt promising that the US was going to produce thousands of new planes this year and thousands more next year, thousands of new tanks this year and thousands more next year. That was encouraging to us and we never really gave up hope that those reinforcements would reach us in time to be effective.

Engineers scraped a dirt runway across the rice paddies next to the village of Cabcaben on the shore of Manila Bay. They also built revetments with banks of dirt 20 feet high around them to protect the new planes, which would be coming from the states. We set up the communications system with a wooden scaffolding; it would be the control tower when Cabcaben Field became operational.

During the daytime, several of us trained our aircrew members on jungle warfare. At night, we would make trips to the shore of Manila Bay and deploy our forces in beach defense exercises. Japanese forces were hammering at our defense lines about eight miles to the north of us, and we could hear the roar from the heavy artillery day and night. Japanese aircraft from Manila across the bay made numerous strafing and bombing attacks on us daily. Throughout the days and nights of January, February, and March, we waited for those supplies and reinforcements from the United States. Many of us had no more protection from the elements than a shelter half spread above our bunks. Everyone lived in tents or outdoors since there were no permanent structures of any kind in the jungle.

Our rations were reduced by half and later to half rations again until men were scrounging over the hills for eatable roots or animals. Some tried iguana, others captured and ate monkeys. There was never enough extra food to overcome the hunger that we suffered constantly.

Malaria, dysentery, and a variety of tropical diseases took their toll until about half of our units were not able to function. When orders came for us to go to the front lines as artillery spotters, Jack Jones and I were flat on our backs with malaria fever. Jay Horowitz and Scott Warner did spot for the artillery until our lines were pushed back, and they were ordered back to our camp.

We continued to live in hope for the arrival of reinforcements to rescue us. There was no other way out. There was no way for us to escape from Bataan, with its barbed wire and bamboo barricades all along the shores and the battle lines across the neck of the peninsula. Bataan was jokingly referred to as the greatest concentration camp in the world. We were captives of our own War Plan Orange III.

US Navy planners had predicted long before World War II that, in the event of war with Japan, it would take two or three years for the US to fight its way across the Pacific to bring relief to the Philippines.[4] Fortunately for us, none of us knew that. But again, that is exactly what happened. It took more than three years for the United States to fight its way back through the Marshall, the Gilbert, and the Mariana islands. These islands, previously occupied by Germany, were given to Japan after World War I under a mandate whereby the Japanese were prohibited from building any military fortifications.

It took three years and four months to rescue the thousands of American soldiers, sailors, and marines who had become victims of WPO III. We had been placed in a totally helpless position because the planners who had developed and supported War Plan Orange III had disregarded the warnings of Generals Embick and Wood.

In retrospect, the only thing that *could* happen under the circumstances *did* happen. Our defensive lines finally gave way to the Japanese forces who had hammered them relentlessly for more than three months.

At Cabcaben Field, on the night of 8 April (Philippine time), we were ordered to withdraw to kilometer post 182, north of Mariveles on the southwestern tip of the Bataan peninsula. We were glad to make the move when we learned that our own heavy artillery guns had taken up positions behind us. It took all night to traverse the eight miles from Cabcaben Field to Mariveles. Again, the road was clogged with vehicles moving very slowly and then stopping for long, unexplained periods of time.

At dawn on 9 April, as we were approaching kilometer post 182, we observed vehicles passing us in the opposite direction and displaying white bedsheets fastened to poles. At first, we could not comprehend. Then we were shocked to realize that the bedsheets were white flags of surrender. In a way, it seemed to bring some relief from the long days, weeks, and months of waiting and worrying. We had endured disease and starvation with no words of encouragement except those repeated promises from President Roosevelt that help was on the way with thousands of planes and tanks. Not one new plane reached us from the United States during the months that we were on Bataan. Not one supply ship reached us from the United States. As the war-weary stragglers made their way into the area where we were ordered to surrender, it appeared to me that it might be feasible to get away from the surrender area and avoid being taken prisoner. I found a couple of my friends, John I. Renka, a B-17 pilot, and Jim Dey, a bombardier, and proposed to them that we try to get away. They both agreed without hesitation.

It was much easier than we anticipated. We casually walked to the road, found a vehicle with the keys still in it, and drove straight to Mariveles harbor without any problem. There we found a small launch with several soldiers aboard and ready to set out to sea. They welcomed us aboard, and we set out for the island of Corregidor, about seven and one-half miles away. It was so easy that I could not believe it was really happening. It was too good to be true. We were escaping from the Bataan peninsula where we had spent more than three months living on hope until we had run out of hope. There were Japanese planes in the sky, but they took no notice of us or our little boat making its way to freedom.

From the dense, malaria-ridden jungles of Bataan, we were headed for Corregidor, that island fortress, bastion of steel and concrete. There was food enough to last for five years and big guns enough to ward off any enemy. There, we would be secure until reinforcements arrived from the United States.

A new problem developed just as we were approaching the shore, however. We observed a flight of Japanese bombers coming from the east like a dark storm blowing up on a sunny day, and it appeared that we would arrive on Corregidor at the same time. Our skipper gave the engine full throttle in the hope that we would make our landing and find shelter just before the bombs exploded on the island.*

Notes

1. In the years before World War I, the War and Navy Departments devised a series of contingency plans wherein a certain color identified the specific plan to be implemented in the event of war with a given country. War Plan Orange (WPO) denoted hostilities with Japan.

From the early 1920s, both the US Army and Navy agreed that the Philippines would prove an early and easy target for a Japanese invasion force. When it came to a Pacific strategy, they agreed upon little else. For its part, the Army urged redeployment of all American forces stationed in the Philippines to a defensive line running from Alaska to Oahu to Panama. Anticipating major sea battles in the Western Pacific and stressing the strategic importance of a Philippine base for offensive operations, the Navy strongly opposed such a move. Following certain other concessions desired by the Army, planners agreed that WPO III would provide at least for the defense of Manila Bay. The authors of WPO III envisioned the defenders of Manila Bay holding out on Bataan and Corregidor for four to six months while the Navy steamed to their relief across the Central Pacific. Significantly, nothing was said about reinforcement of the Army garrison or how long it might take the Navy to fight its way back to the Philippines.

Shortly after WPO III went into effect, the "color plans," each of which envisioned US hostilities with only a single country, were transformed into the Rainbow series which more realistically assumed the existence of various combinations of alliances and multiple theaters of war. The terms of Rainbow 5 most closely approximated the situation that existed when the US entered World War II. However, although WPO III had been superseded by Rainbow 5, the provisions and assumptions of the former were incorporated into the latter. Thus, as a practical matter, the third revision of WPO III, written in 1938, was in effect when the Japanese bombed Pearl Harbor and attacked the Philippines. More importantly, although no one in Washington cared to admit it, there was no change in the prevailing

---

*Continued by Chapter 17, "Corregidor."

assumption that the Philippines could not be held against a determined Japanese foe. Wesley Frank Craven and James Lea Cate, eds., *The Army Air Forces in World War II*, vol. 1, *Plans and Early Operations* (Chicago: University of Chicago Press, 1948–1958), 139–48; D. Clayton James, *The Years of MacArthur, 1941–1945*, vol. 2 (Boston: Houghton Mifflin, 1975), 13, 26–30, 34–37, 86; and Ronald H. Spector, *Eagle Against the Sun: The American War with Japan* (New York: Free Press, 1985), chap. 3. See also Louis Morton, "War Plan Orange: Evolution of a Strategy," *World Politics* 11 (January 1959): 221–50 (see especially p. 248).

2. Embick's opposition to defending the Philippines is discussed in Morton, 237, and in Spector, 58–59.

3. Spector, 56.

4. Contemporary estimates of the time it would take in the event of war with Japan to establish US naval supremacy in the Western Pacific and ship reinforcements to the Philippines are noted in Morton, 241.

Carl R. Wildner

On 18 April 1942, classmates Carl Wildner and Harry McCool sat in their planes on the deck of the aircraft carrier USS *Hornet* in the far western Pacific Ocean. In the plane in front of Wildner, at the controls of his B-25 Billy Mitchell bomber, sat the most famous flyer in the world. James ("Jimmie") Harold Doolittle had won the Thompson Trophy, the Bendix Trophy, the Spirit of St. Louis Award, the MacKay Trophy, and the Harmon Trophy. No other American pilot had amassed so many flying honors. In addition to all of this, he had been the first to fly an outside loop (1928); the first to take off, fly a set course, and land "blind" without ever seeing the ground (1929); and the first to cross the US in less than 12 hours.

No daredevil, seat-of-the-pants flyer, was this Lt Col Jimmie Doolittle. He had taken his flight training in the United States Army Air Corps. Then in 1925 he had earned his doctor of science degree in aeronautical engineering from Massachusetts Institute of Technology. No person was better qualified to lead the first aerial raid on the homeland of the Japanese.

World War II was four months and 10 days old. The Japanese had swept across the southwest Pacific to take Hong Kong, Manila, Singapore, Java, Wake Island, Guam, and a host of other islands approaching Australia. Bataan had fallen. General MacArthur had escaped from the Philippines one month earlier. That left us in the Philippines as the only organized military forces which had thus far withstood the might of the Japanese onslaught.

US military leaders had been frustrated that the Japanese had achieved such success. Yet there seemed no way for US bombers to reach the mainland of Japan. Our B-17 bombers, which had held the high hopes for leading the American aerial offensive, had been riddled and driven back to Australia. Moreover, the Japanese were bombing air bases there. Of the original 35 B-17s in the Philippines at the outbreak of the war, less than 10 were operational after four months of war. The plane did not have the range to bomb Japan and return to any Allied base. There seemed to be no way to retaliate against the Japanese—no way to bomb their homeland.

President Franklin Roosevelt was not willing to admit defeat. Two weeks after the Japanese attack on Pearl Harbor, he issued a courageous order to his Air Corps. It was, "Bomb Japan!" It was a daring proposal that would have been considered impossible by most enlightened airmen of the day. It took an ingenious naval operations officer, Capt Francis S. Low, to come up with a workable idea. He determined that it would be possible for planes to take off from an aircraft carrier, bomb Japan, and fly to a landing field in China. At first, the plan seemed like an impossible dream, but the captain worked it out in careful detail.

Sixteen crews, which included Carl Wildner and Harry McCool, practiced short-field takeoffs at Eglin Field, Florida. Their B-25s had been modified under the careful scrutiny of their chief, Jimmie Doolittle. Each prepared to carry two 500-pound bombs and 1,000 pounds of incendiary bombs. Extra fuel included five-gallon cans of gasoline to be poured into the main tanks while in flight. The highly sophisticated Norden bombsight was unacceptable. Instead a simple gadget which cost 20 cents was used because it was more suitable for their type of low-altitude bombing.[1]

After three weeks of training, including only 20 to 30 hours of actual flying time, the crews took their planes to Alameda, California. There they loaded them aboard the newly commissioned aircraft carrier *Hornet*. When 16 B-25s and their five-man crews were aboard the *Hornet* and at sea, their mission was officially announced. It was a thrilling moment with cheers ringing from every section of the carrier. All crew members were given the option of leaving the mission with no questions asked. None accepted the offer though they knew they would be engaged in an extremely dangerous mission. None of the crew members had ever taken off from an aircraft carrier in a B-25. In fact, not one had so much as seen it done.

The *Hornet* was not alone on the mission. It was supported by the largest force the Navy could put together in the Pacific at that time. Designated as Task Force Sixteen and commanded

80

by Admiral William F. ("Bull") Halsey, the force contained another 15 ships including four cruisers, eight destroyers, two oilers, and the aircraft carrier, USS *Enterprise.*

The plan was to rendezvous in mid-Pacific on 12 April. Then the task force would move to within 400 miles of Japan in the evening so that the bombers would be over Tokyo at sunset. After dropping their bombs, navigators would direct their aircraft by celestial navigation over the 2,000 miles to secret bases on the Chinese mainland.

The task force was headed west when those carefully laid plans exploded. At eight o'clock on Saturday morning, 18 April 1942, the Americans sighted an enemy surface ship. There could be no doubt that it had alerted the mainland forces of the approach of a huge US flotilla. A successful attack on Task Force Sixteen would destroy the effectiveness of the US Navy in the Pacific. The decision was to sink the Japanese ship, launch the aircraft, and withdraw the naval ships immediately.

Long before their scheduled take-off time, the crews hurriedly mounted their aircraft. Wildner held his breath as he watched the plane immediately in front of him rev up its engines to full throttle. It had the least runway because it was the first in line. The air was charged with excitement as the crews watched their leader. With a roar, Jimmie Doolittle's plane rolled across the deck of the carrier and out over the windswept sea. The mission had started successfully.

Next was Wildner's turn. Would his pilot, Lt Travis Hoover, with only a fraction of the experience and expertise of the great Jimmie Doolittle, be able to emulate the veteran flyer? In seconds he would know the answer. Lieutenant Wildner stood in the aisle between Hoover and copilot Richard Miller as the engines roared. They waited for the Navy flagman to give the signal so they would reach the take-off point when the bow of the *Hornet* was at a high point above the water. Wildner had little time to think about it. The plane was moving down the deck and lifting off over the forbidding, choppy waters of the Pacific and on its way to bomb Tokyo. In the second plane after Wildner, came his classmate, Harry McCool. One by one the flyers moved their aircraft into position, revved up, waited for the flag, and then felt those uneasy moments as the plane hung uncertainly between the water and the sky.

At 0940 in the morning, 16 B-25 planes were rushing toward Japan to do something that had never been done before. Not one of them could have grasped the significance of this rendezvous with destiny.

Instead of taking off at a point 400 miles from Japan, the flyers were more than 620 miles from their targets.[2] That meant that instead of dropping their bombs in the evening, as previously planned, they would arrive over their targets at midday. Then came the nagging question of whether there would be enough fuel to reach their destination in China. In less than three hours they would arrive over the island empire of Japan.

The city of Tokyo had concluded its routine Saturday air raid drill, and people were resuming their usual Saturday chores. Though they had been at war in China for many years, no enemy plane had ever found its way to the skies above Tokyo. So when the American planes roared over the city, many mistook them for a show in connection with the Saturday air raid drill.

As his plane raced toward the city of Tokyo, Wildner was unable to identify his intended target; so the crew unloaded their bombs on a factory building. Smoke bellowed into the air as pilot Hoover pushed the throttles forward and nosed the plane down to tree-top level to avoid Japanese fighters. Soon they were flying over Tokyo Bay just above the waves at top speed. Ahead to his right, Wildner spotted Jimmie Doolittle's plane heading for the China coast.

With the bombing part of the raid behind him, Wildner turned his attention to the gasoline gauges. A moment's calculation told him that the plane would not reach its destination unless they had a tailwind. In addition to navigating the plane, it was his duty to transfer gas from some of the 10 five-gallon cans into the 50-gallon tank located in the bottom gun turret.

The afternoon clouds thickened into a completely overcast sky as the day wore on. Then came rain squalls making it impossible to navigate other than by dead reckoning. There were no radio, radar, or celestial observations to assist with the navigational problems. The frequency of the station they had planned to home in on was dead. Wildner stood in his favorite position between the pilot and copilot and watched the gas gauges move steadily but surely toward the empty mark. He strained his eyes trying to penetrate the late afternoon haze to see land. Then suddenly he sighted a patch of land far off to the right side of the plane. He was able to identify it as an island at the mouth of the Yangtze River. Shortly thereafter the starboard engine coughed a couple of times and quit. The copilot quickly revived it with the fuel pump. At that point the crew saw the dim outline of the mainland ahead. As they crossed the shoreline, pilot Hoover realized that he had to gain more altitude or be faced with a crash landing. When he nosed the plane up, the right engine cut out again. Then he realized that he was faced with a serious problem. He needed to find a place to set the plane down.

It was drizzling rain and almost dark when he found a rice paddy. All hands prepared for a crash landing. There again Hoover's skill as a pilot paid off. With wheels up, the plane hit the ground and skidded along the muddy field with minimal damage. The crew scrambled out. It had been more than 10 hours since the crew had lifted off from the *Hornet*. Being safely on the ground was a welcome relief from the day's tense excitement though they had little idea of their next move.

The pilot decided to destroy the aircraft so it would not fall into enemy hands. Flames lit up the entire countryside and caused alarm that Japanese soldiers might be attracted to the scene. The crew quickly moved to the top of a hill where they watched and waited throughout the night. They remained in the same location the following day until dark. Then they started the long trip to Chungking.

On the third day of travel they came upon a Chinese house where a teenaged boy and two women gave them food and drink. They learned by sign language that they were in friendly territory. There were no Japanese soldiers in the vicinity.

On 22 April, they arrived at Sunchway. From there they traveled the long, long road to Chungking via sedan chair, bus, and airplane.

The Doolittle Raid was only the beginning of Wildner's wartime experiences. On his way back to the United States, he flew from China across the Burma Hump to Delhi, India. There he learned that navigators were needed in the India-Burma area. The situation was desperate because Japanese forces were moving through Burma toward India. Instead of returning to the United States, he was assigned as a B-25 crew member flying missions against the Japanese.

Carl Wildner was based at Chalsulia, 113 miles west of Calcutta. From there he flew bombing missions to central Burma. He survived numerous raids against railway and industrial targets but his planes were sometimes damaged by flak. After he had flown 25 missions, someone in the War Department decided that as a Doolittle Raider he should not be flying over enemy territory. He returned to the US where he remained in the Air Force until 1954.

Notes

1. Designed by Capt C. R. Greening, the Raiders' armament officer, and consisting merely of two pieces of aluminum, this rudimentary bombsight proved quite effective at altitudes of 1,500 feet or below. Wesley Frank Craven and James Lea Cate, eds., *The Army Air Forces in World War II*, vol. 1, *Plans and Early Operations* (Chicago: University of Chicago Press, 1948–1958), 439.

2. Doolittle hoped to launch his planes when the *Hornet* was within 450 miles of the Japanese coast. Unfortunately, the task force was spotted by a small Japanese picket ship while still steaming some 200 miles east of the desired launching point. To prevent a preemptive strike by Japanese naval air, Doolittle and task force commander Vice Adm William F. Halsey agreed on an immediate takeoff. Craven and Cate, 441.

Harry McCool

Harry McCool's plane did not have the smooth takeoff from the *Hornet* that Wildner had enjoyed. There was trouble from the start. With 12 planes impatiently waiting behind, the starboard engine refused to start. There were anxious moments as it sputtered and fumed for what seemed like a long time. It finally fired up and sent the B-25 plummeting along the deck and out over the water. The crew circled the carrier one time and noted that the many ships which had escorted them were steaming eastward to get out of danger of being attacked by the Japanese.

On the flight toward Tokyo the crew members received the disconcerting word that the rear gun turret was not functioning. That told them that there was no protection in the event they were attacked from the rear. In addition to that problem, they learned that their left wing tank was leaking precious fuel.

Lieutenant Holstrom, the pilot, instructed McCool to plot a course that would bring the plane to the south part of Tokyo. Their hearts beat a little faster when they sighted some small islands telling them that they were nearing their target.

Then in a flash, they observed two pursuit planes flying directly toward them. Pilot Holstrom made an abrupt turn and passed below the fighters just as tracer machine-gun bullets arched across the sky above the B-25. The pilot's split-second maneuver saved the plane. Then came two more fighter planes bearing in at about 1,500 feet above them. Holstrom had instructed the bombardier to salvo the entire bomb load in the event of an enemy attack before reaching their target. This he did at about 75 feet above the ground traveling at 270 miles per hour. Again, pilot Holstrom outmaneuvered the attacking planes by abruptly turning below them. Then Harry McCool took up his heading for the secret base in China.

Like Wildner, he found that navigating became more difficult as the bomber proceeded toward China. He was able to take a couple of lines of position with his octant. Then for a while he was able to take bearings on Radio Tokyo. The sky became overcast and before the airmen reached the China coast it began raining. Visibility was zero and there was no response on the radio frequency that was supposed to have been available for them in China. The frequency was dead.

What the airmen did not know was that the communications with the Chinese forces in the area had been badly snarled up even before the flight. It was doubtful that preparations for the arrival of the Doolittle Raiders in China had ever been completed.

Generalissimo Chiang Kai-shek had been vehemently opposed to the operation from the beginning. He was fearful of retaliation by the Japanese forces against the civilian population in the area. As will be seen, his fears were well founded.

The rainy night blackened into hopelessness, and there was no help for the flyers. With no navigational aids other than the compass, there was no way to find a landing field in the dark. So with the fuel supply almost exhausted, there was only one thing to do. A crash landing was out of the question because they could not see the mountainous terrain below them. They had to leave the aircraft.

Pilot Holstrom gave the order and then held a steady course as first one and then another of the crew members dropped out into the dark Chinese sky. Harry was the third crew member to go. He first checked his harness to be sure that it was secure. Then he jumped. The second that he felt that he was clear of the plane, he jerked the rip cord. The impact of the parachute harness on his body brought a shock to his entire system. Much later he learned that he had cracked a vertebra in the process.

In a very short time Harry hit the ground. The crew members had jumped from 6,000 feet but the mountains had not been far below them. He quickly realized that his parachute was tangled in some shrubbery and that he was on a mountainside. He wrapped his legs around the base of a tree to avoid sliding down the steep mountainside. With each movement of his body, rocks would become dislodged and go tumbling down. He could hear them for a time and then there would be silence. Then he would hear them again far below. He could see nothing, but from the sounds he concluded that he was over a steep precipice. There was nothing to do but to wrap some of the parachute cloth around himself for warmth and wait for dawn.

The first light of the new day showed McCool only that he was in the mountains somewhere in China. There were no signs of the airplane or any of the crew members. He had little idea of his location or which way to start traveling to find his way to Chungking where the surviving members were supposed to rendezvous. He knew two things for certain: the date was 19 April 1942, and it was his 24th birthday. He was to celebrate it alone.

He disengaged himself from the parachute harness, carefully edged himself to more secure terrain, and started the long, painful journey down the mountain. So rugged was the terrain and so painful was his journey that he took three days to reach the bottom of the mountain. A rushing stream helped his progress as he waded in and was bounced from boulder to boulder for long distances.

Finally, the stream fed into a river when he reached a valley. There he was able to locate a friendly Chinese family. They did not speak or understand English, but they happily provided the flyer with food and shelter. On the fourth day, a couple of Chinese soldiers arrived and transported him by chair car to Chinyun in Fukien Province.

In two days, a couple of his crew members joined him. Then the three of them made contact with a Catholic missionary priest known as Father Joyce. He was the first English-speaking person any of them had encountered since leaving the aircraft carrier *Hornet*.

Father Joyce introduced the flyers to the local governmental officials. There was much merriment when the crew members told of the Doolittle Raid on the Japanese mainland. Then the flyers were feted to a week-long series of dinners, receptions, and parades in celebration of the raid. They were given a real hero's welcome by the Chinese people.

The local officials did not know that the Japanese army had dispatched hundreds of troops to the area in one of the greatest and most brutal manhunts in history. Otherwise the celebration would have been short-lived. Chang Kai-shek's worst fears of retaliation were well founded. It was said that 53 battalions of Japanese soldiers descended upon Chekiang Province. They slaughtered men, women, and children in areas where the American flyers had traveled. Entire villages were burned to the ground, and all of the landing fields in the area were plowed up and destroyed.

It was estimated that a quarter of a million people were massacred in three months after the Doolittle Raid. The raiders themselves were fortunate. With assistance of brave and friendly Chinese allies, all but eight of the 80 flyers were able to evade capture by the Japanese.[1]

McCool and his fellow crew members evaded the Japanese. Traveling by charcoal powered bus, boat, and train to a Chinese army headquarters, they had a joyful reunion with Jimmie Doolittle and other survivors of the Raid. Then by train and plane they moved on to Chungking, the wartime headquarters of the Chinese government.

There Madame Chiang Kai-shek and the Generalissimo personally awarded each of the flyers with the order of the Celestial Cloud, Grade A, Class II. In addition, the US government awarded each of its heroes the Distinguished Flying Cross.

With his newly acquired awards, McCool, like his classmate Wildner, flew B-25 missions over Burma. Thirteen turned out to be his unlucky number. Less than two months after the Tokyo raid and on his 13th mission, his plane was hit. It crashed into the sea 50 miles off the coast in the Bay of Bengal near Akyab, Burma. All crew members survived except the photographer. McCool suffered a laceration on his face, a broken nose, and a deep cut in his leg.

For days the airmen drifted in a rubber lifeboat. The evening breeze caused the raft to drift in toward the shore. Then the morning breeze would carry it back to sea until the fifth day when they finally reached the shore. A C-47 transport plane arrived from Dum Dum Field, Calcutta and flew them back to their base. After hospitalization and recuperation, McCool returned to the US via Africa and the South Atlantic.

In Oklahoma City, Harry McCool was again elevated to hero status at the City Civic Center where the governor, senators, and other dignitaries recognized his exploits. There were photograph sessions and interviews. Later came orders to cross the South Atlantic again on 2 January 1944. McCool was on his way to England as the navigator of a B-26 Marauder bomber where he would fly 45 missions against the Germans. There he led the 344th Bomb Group on raids against German submarine pens and V-1 and V-2 sites along the coast of France and Holland.

D day, 6 June 1944, found him navigating missions against antilanding obstacles on the Normandy beachhead. He continued flying missions until the end of the war.

Notes

1. Fifteen of the 16 B-25s flown by the Raiders crash-landed in China. (The 16th plane landed in Vladivostok where the crew was interned by the Russians.) Of the eight captured Raiders, three were executed and the remaining five were sentenced to life imprisonment. As noted by the author, thousands of Chinese were murdered by the Japanese in the wake of the Doolittle Raid. Japanese wrath was focused on Chekiang Province where most of the B-25s crash-landed. Wesley Frank Craven and James Lea Cate, eds., *The Army Air Forces in World War II*, vol. 1, *Plans and Early Operations* (Chicago: University of Chicago Press, 1948–1958), 442; Geoffrey Perret, *Winged Victory: The Army Air Forces in World War II* (New York: Random House, 1993), 152–53.

Merrill Kern Gordon, Jr.

Bette Deardorff was at home from Washington State University when she met a handsome lieutenant in the Air Corps by the name of Merrill Kern Gordon. They began to date and were married five months later on 27 November 1941. Their plans for a honeymoon were quickly squelched when Gordon's commanding officer turned down his request for leave. Gordon later learned that he was on special secret orders "Plum" to fly across the Pacific Ocean to Clark Field in the Philippine Islands.

Half of his bombardment group including his classmate, Homer Taylor, took off for Hawaii on 6 December just in time to land in the midst of the Japanese attack on Pearl Harbor on 7 December 1941. After that attack, plans changed. The B-17s could not safely travel to the Philippines via Hawaii. Instead Gordon would have to fly the eastern route by way of South America, Africa, India, and Java. So Gordon flew to MacDill Field at Tampa, Florida, in preparation for the "round the world" flight to the Philippines.

At the stroke of midnight on 31 December 1941, Gordon's mighty B-17 roared down the runway at MacDill Field. Then it headed out on the long uncertain route that would take it to the Far East. There was an air of excitement mixed with melancholy as copilot Lt Rowan ("Judge") Thomas picked up the microphone and bade the tower operator a "Happy New Year!" and the plane faded into the darkness of the night. Stops on the island of Trinidad, Belém on the Amazon River, and Natal in Brazil were routine.

Natal was the jumping off place for the flight across the South Atlantic Ocean to the coast of Africa. That was the flight that would test all of the navigational skills Gordon had learned from Charlie Lunn back in Coral Gables. There would be no radio aids to navigation and no landmarks to check his position. Weather reports were unreliable because meteorological services were limited at that stage of the war. There were only the stars, the clouds, and water, water, and more water in every direction. He had only his trusty octant to guide the plane through the night. The plane took off from Natal just before dark, climbed to flight altitude, and the crew began to settle down for the long flight when a new element of concern entered the scene. One of the engines began to run irregularly then coughed and stopped. At that point there was nothing to do but to turn back to Natal. There they were greeted by the surprised detachment of US Marines who had seen them off just a short time before. Mechanics repaired the engine so that it worked perfectly and the eager crew headed out for a second try at the 12-hour trip to Africa.

A glorious new world opened for the crew when they reached flight altitude. There they flew along seemingly suspended between the wide Atlantic Ocean far below and the magnificent sky full of stars above. Gordon pointed out the Southern Cross which everybody had heard about but none had seen before. Other constellations were unfamiliar even to Gordon as he picked out first one star and then another to plot his course. Then, as seems to happen all too often on a celestial navigation mission, clouds began to blot out the stars until the sky was as black as the sea below.

The weatherman at Natal had told them that they might be in a storm for some 500 miles along the course, but he had thought that they would pass to the south of it. At the beginning of the flight, the crew members were certain that there would be no storm because the skies had been clear as far as they could see. Later they had passed through more and more rolling, black clouds. Bright flashes of lightning filled the sky, and they knew that they were in a South Atlantic storm. The plane was being tossed about like a cork on a rough sea. The pilots flew on instruments as heavy rain pelted the windows and fuselage of the aircraft. Thunder roared as the plane's altimeter showed that they were being swept up and down as much as 200 feet at a time in spite of all efforts by the pilots to hold a straight and level course. As the storm grew in intensity, there was only one thing to do and that was to try to climb above it. Crew members struggled to get into their sheepskin-lined flight suits and their oxygen masks. Then at 22,000 feet the plane came out of the clouds and into the smooth, clear, blue heavens above the storm. The crew had its first baptism of a tropical storm at sea. There would be more, many more, but now they were veterans. They knew that they could survive.

The engines of the plane droned on until the light of a new day broke. Weary eyes looked out across the peaceful sea for some sign of land. Almost 12 hours had passed since their departure from Natal. Seeing no land, the copilot began to get concerned that their fuel supply was getting low and might not hold out until they reached Africa. Moments later Gordon comforted the crew by giving his estimated time of arrival. As they came within minutes of the time that they should be making landfall, there was still no land in sight. For a moment they were excited at the sight of a smudge on the horizon, but were dismayed to learn that it was only a dark low-hanging cloud. Seconds later, Cape St. Queens loomed up through the morning haze dead ahead of the aircraft. They were within sight of their destination. Gordon's navigation had been perfect.

They had crossed the Atlantic Ocean and survived a severe storm at sea. All that remained was to find the landing field. They found one but observed that another B-17 was already there with its wheels mired in the soft asphalt of the runway. As they were studying that situation, they were suddenly alarmed at the sight of a fighter plane bearing in on them from seven o'clock. There was good reason to be alarmed because they knew two squadrons of German Messerschmitts were based within flying range of their destination. On orders from the plane commander, the sergeant manning the twin .50-caliber machine guns in the top turret turned the guns on the intruder. Everyone was relieved when the fighter came around parallel to their course and revealed Royal Air Force markings. They had a friend. The RAF pilot dipped his wings and indicated that he would lead them to the proper landing field. They followed the escort and landed their plane to finish the first big leg of their journey to support the beleaguered Air Corps in the Philippines.

But all was not well. As the front wheels felt the asphalt of the runway and the plane settled down, the tail wheel collapsed. Eight feet of the tail section broke loose. The crew had not realized that the aircraft had been damaged during the takeoff from the rough runway at Natal 12 hours before. They had flown 1,800 miles and passed through a horrendous storm in an aircraft that was structurally unsound. But they were on land, safe, and thankful to God for that.

It did not take long for the crew to learn that there were no spare parts for the new B-17 anywhere along the western coast of Africa. Much to their consternation, the airmen received orders to abandon their plane and return to the United States to get a new one. Apparently their efforts to reach the Philippines were doomed. Weeks had passed since they had first started their trip, and now the discouraged crew was going back to start over. They boarded a Pan American clipper in Lagos, Nigeria, and flew back across the Atlantic, landing at the Pan American clipper base at La Guardia Field, New York. From there they went back to Tampa, Florida, to restart their trip in a brand new B-17.

The happy side of the story was that while they were waiting in Tampa for delivery of their new plane, Gordon's bride was able to join him for their much-delayed honeymoon. But, all too quickly their time in Tampa came to an end. This time the crew's destination was different. American forces had been driven from Clark Field and the Philippines and were regrouping in Australia. Gordon was assigned to a unit of six B-17s scheduled to fly to a base in China. From there they would bomb the islands of Japan. Soon they would be in the war.

The six planes flew by individual navigation back across the blue Caribbean Sea, over the wide jungles of Brazil, and then to Natal for their hop across the Atlantic Ocean. This time Gordon's crew was experienced and had a newborn confidence. They would cross the ocean, the deserts of North Africa, and the Middle East to China to do something that had never been done before. They would bomb the islands of Japan. Members of the crew had no way of knowing that Jimmie Doolittle and his band of flyers were also heading for Japan from the other side of the world.

When the flyers reached Calcutta, India, they were advised that the Japanese forces had captured Rangoon, Burma. Thus, they had to delay their plans to fly to China. They were given orders to prepare for a bombing mission from Karachi against the Japanese shipping and the dock facilities of Rangoon.

The crews loaded each of their planes with gasoline and 14 300-pound bombs. They had endured much danger since they first started to the Philippines, but now they faced a new kind of danger. How would the crew perform under combat conditions? They were well acquainted with each other, but they would be operating under new conditions in the days ahead. At their briefing they learned that their first combat mission would be at night. Moreover, they would be flying over the target at an altitude of only 3,500 feet to drop flares. The flares would illuminate the target for two other planes flying in at different altitudes. Then their plane would return over the target to drop its bombs.

The B-17 churned through the dark of night for six and one-half hours. The crew had flown together for thousands of miles, but this was different. They were on their first bombing mission. In half an hour they would be over the target. The pilots were comforted when a quarter-moon came up over the hazy horizon, knowing that Gordon could "shoot" it with his octant and give them a line of position. A foggy haze below the plane made it difficult to tell whether they were over land or water until the copilot was able to make out the meandering of a river below them.

When Gordon informed the pilots that they were approaching the target, there was some doubt because they observed another plane dropping flares about 20 miles to the south. With that, the pilot turned and headed in the direction of the flares.

"No," shouted Gordon, "That is not it."

In a matter of seconds they knew that Gordon was right. Suddenly the whole sky lit up with flashing searchlights zeroing in on the plane. They were over the target. They dropped their flares and made an abrupt turn in an effort to get away from the beam of the searchlights. Puffs of antiaircraft fire were all about them as they maneuvered violently to get away from the area and climb to altitude to drop their bomb load.

The bomb run at a much higher altitude was easy compared to going in over the target area at 3,500 feet with the flares. After dropping their bombs, they were able to relax for the long ride from Rangoon back to Karachi. The crew had worked together magnificently for their first mission in combat.

There were more missions over Burma during the months of March, April, and May 1942 in support of Gen Joseph ("Vinegar Joe") Stilwell's forces. Their mission was to stop the advance of the Japanese in Burma. But there arose another serious threat facing the Allied forces in the war. In North Africa, the brilliant "Desert Fox," Gen Erwin Rommel, had advanced to El Alamein about one hundred miles from Cairo. In addition to that, German forces were at Baku, USSR, and were about to break south around the Caspian Sea in a giant pincer movement against the Suez Canal. The seriousness of the situation required the movement of bombers from India to the Middle East. For Gordon, that meant a move from India to Lydda, Palestine, a short distance from Tel Aviv. From there he flew numerous missions through the months of July, August, and September against the German-held cities of Tobruk, Benghazi, Tripoli, and Naples. There were also bombing missions against shipping in the Mediterranean Sea attempting to resupply General Rommel.

By December 1942, the port city of Tobruk had been captured by the Allies. Gordon's squadron moved there to carry out missions against the Italian port cities of Brendisi, Messina, and Naples.

Then came an unusual special assignment in which Gordon was to navigate a B-24 bomber, with electronic gear operated by a RAF radio operator, to ferret out German radar sites along the coast of Italy. The purpose was to find blank spots in German and Italian radar coverage so that Allied bombing missions could be routed through them. The first such mission over southern Italy was so successful that another much more demanding mission was planned. This mission was expected to take about 16 hours (mostly at night) to fly across Crete, Greece, Trieste, east of the Alps, then south along the western coast to Rome. From there the B-24 would fly east over Greece to Crete then back to base at Tobruk.

The mission worked like clockwork as Gordon carefully charted his course and the RAF radio operator plotted the location of various radar sites along the way. Under any other conditions, the flight could have been a fantastic journey over the Greek Islands and along the Italian coast to the Alps. In wartime the sense of beauty was crowded out as anxious eyes scanned the dark skies for enemy planes. From time to time, there were menacing bursts of antiaircraft fire reaching up through the darkness. At one point, the crew thought the bomber had been hit, but the plane continued churning on through the night seemingly unscathed.

Dawn was breaking as the airmen crossed the rugged mountains of Greece. They had flown 12 hours of their 16-hour mission, and they knew that the worst was over. All that remained was to settle down for the long monotonous ride across Greece and the Mediterranean Sea to their home base. But, the peaceful drowsiness of the crew was shattered when all four engines suddenly cut out. The plane was dropping out of the sky until an alert crew chief quickly switched back to fuel tanks that were considered to have been emptied. Miraculously the engines were restarted. At some point along the way, a fuel line had been severed or a tank ruptured causing the loss of all of their gasoline except that which remained in the bottom of the tanks they had been using. The pilot knew that the little gas remaining would sustain their flight for only a limited time. Thus, the engine restart was only a short reprieve from catastrophe. There was no likelihood that they could reach their base at Tobruk far across the Mediterranean Sea.

Crew members checked their parachute harnesses and prepared to bail out or to ditch, whichever the plane commander ordered. Gordon, on orders from the captain, plotted a course to Turkey, the nearest neutral country which they might possibly reach before their fuel ran out. As they approached the Turkish shore, they discovered a long, sandy beach where they could bring the plane down. All was well as they settled down for an apparently perfect landing, but near the end of their roll, the nose wheel hit a ditch and collapsed. That was the only real damage to the plane. No member of the crew was injured in the landing, but with the nose wheel gone there was no way to get the plane back in the air.

As the crew members surveyed the damage and speculated on their next move, local farmers appeared. They stood back cautiously at first. When they observed no hostility, they moved in closer. Then came the police. After some routine questioning, the police knew nothing to do but to turn the flyers over to the military. The army in turn loaded the flyers onto a train and transported them to Ankara, the capital city of Turkey. Having just arrived from the hot deserts of North Africa, the flyers were surprised and poorly prepared for the cold weather and snow that awaited them at their destination.

Their military escort lodged them in an old apartment building about one-half mile from the center of the city. Some 30 interned Russian soldiers occupied the third story of the building while 20 American and British internees were quartered on the second floor. Gordon's room was furnished with two cots and a small table. A Turkish guard stood in the hallway near a fireplace. That fireplace was the only source of heat for the second floor of the building. Gordon was able to write to Bette to tell her that he was safe and in good health, but because of censorship his efforts to tell of his whereabouts were blotted out of the letter.

The flyers were pleased to learn that the Turkish people would be friendly and helpful to them. Upon signing a permit form, they were able to travel about the city with certain limitations. They were informed that the Turkish government would abide by the Geneva Conference Agreement as it pertained to prisoners of war and internees. It would provide the internees with 36 dollars per month for food and 60 cents a day for spending money.

It was a strange world for the flyers though they had lived in strange surroundings since they had left the States. The clothes worn by many of the Turkish men were like baggy pantaloons. Food was different. Gordon soon learned that he could purchase a loaf of bread from a local vendor who appeared at the open market across the street with his load of bread on his donkey. Gordon would then trade half of the loaf at a food stand for a plate consisting of figs, rice, and mutton. It was not what he would have ordered in a restaurant at home, but it sustained him in this strange new environment.

The crew had no idea how long they were to be held as internees in Turkey. All they knew was that their busy activities of the past year had come to a quick end. They had flown bombing missions one after another month after month, all the way from Rangoon to many of the German-held ports on the Mediterranean Sea. They had flown through seas of ugly puffs of antiaircraft fire, and they had watched anxiously as streams of machine-gun bullets sprayed past their aircraft. They had experienced all of the terror and ugliness of war. That had ended abruptly. They reposed in a peaceful neutral country far away from it all. How long would they be here? How long would it last?

From the moment they had arrived in Ankara, there had been rumors of repatriation, a prisoner exchange, or release. The flyers could hear anything they wanted to believe. Days turned into weeks and weeks into months. It was an interesting life, but what the flyers wanted more than anything else was to get back to their outfit. Their biggest problem was that there was no one authority to which they could look for sound, reliable information.

Then abruptly one day it happened! They were going to be released! An exchange of internees had been worked out between the German and British embassies. Fifty internees from the Allied forces were being exchanged for a like number of Axis internees. Gordon and his crew would go back to their bomb group which was located at Benghazi at that time. For Merrill Kern Gordon days of flying combat missions were not over. It would be necessary for him to fly two more missions before he would be eligible to return to the US.

One evening in May 1943 when Bette Gordon returned home from her employment at the bank, she was delighted to find another letter from her husband. But this was not just another letter. It was the good news she had been waiting for. Gordon was back with his outfit. He had just two more missions to fly, then he would be coming home!

Then one day in late May, Bette received a phone call from New York City. It was Gordon. He had flown his last two missions, flown back across the south Atlantic and then to New York. Arrangements were that he would take the train to Great Falls, Montana. Bette would go there to wait for him. Gordon was no longer the carefree lieutenant Bette had met so many months before. He had endured all of the horrors of aerial warfare, navigated bombing missions, and survived barrages of Japanese, Italian, and German antiaircraft fire on three continents.

Gordon wound up his military career in World War II at Tampa, Florida, training new aircrew members for combat. Upon leaving the military, he and Bette moved to Winfield, Kansas, where Gordon established a successful manufacturing business.

Francis B. Rang

The skies over Sicily are a clear light blue, without a cloud to be seen anywhere—except over majestic 10,700-foot Mt. Etna. The waves of the deep blue Mediterranean Sea lap incessantly against the shores as they have done for thousands of years. It seems that the whole world is at peace.

It was not so in July of 1943. The Allied forces had suffered one setback after another in the desert battles of North Africa. The Axis forces had been on the move until the Allies had stopped Gen Erwin Rommel's Afrika Korps at El Alamein, Egypt. From that time, the tide of the war in Africa had turned. By May 1943, the last German forces in Africa had surrendered to the Allies.

The island of Sicily was vital because of its strategic location between Africa and Europe. Once conquered, it could become a springboard to Italy and southern Europe.

War was not new to the island. The Normans, the French, the Austrians, the Greeks, the Carthaginians, the Romans, and the Saracens had all invaded Sicily in previous wars. It had seen invasions by soldiers in wooden ships with galley slaves chained to their positions at the oars. It had seen soldiers wearing heavy mail armor bearing swords and spears. However, the year of 1943 brought a new kind of warrior. Soldiers by the hundreds came ashore in heavily armored landing craft while others descended from the sky in gliders and parachutes.

There was yet another new kind of soldier dressed in heavy, sheepskin-lined, brown-leather suits. He rode on an airborne platform being propelled by four gasoline engines. On each such platform was a team of 11 men and a load of ten 500-pound bombs. The platform was encased in a thin aluminum capsule. It carried the designation of the B-24D Liberator bomber.

At 0800, on 10 July, Maj Francis Bernard Rang took off from a north African airfield as navigator on such an aircraft.

His mission was to bomb the vital railroad station at Messina, Sicily. The flight had taken a little more than four hours when the bombers headed on a course of 45 degrees at 21,500 feet. They would remain on that heading for 70 seconds, drop their bombs, and then get away from the target area.

In the clear Sicilian skies, they could see the city of Messina and the railroad yards far below. The toe of the boot of Italy was across the two-mile wide Strait of Messina to their right side. There was not an enemy fighter plane to be seen in any direction. It would be an easy bomb run under ideal conditions.

Rang had been on many bombing missions and, in the two years since he had been commissioned as a navigator, he had advanced through the ranks of first lieutenant and captain to the rank of major in the 389th Bombardment Group. The story of how he found his way from his home in Williamsburg, Virginia, into the nose of a bomber over Europe is the same as the story of thousands of boys from every state in the Union during World War II. He wanted to fly. He wanted to be a part of the US Army Air Corps. He was there.

He could have been taken for a movie actor in one of the early aviation movies. He was tall, handsome, and soft-spoken, with dark hair and dark eyes. But in their bulky, brown, leather flying suits and helmets, the flyers all looked alike. The suits were necessary because, even though they were over the Mediterranean Sea, the temperature was freezing cold at 21,500 feet.

The bomb run was going according to schedule. The crew was not disturbed to see puffs of smoke well below their altitude as they approached the bomb release point with just 17 seconds to go. They had all been through it many times before. They knew the routine well. The puffs of smoke from the antiaircraft grew in intensity as they reached the bomb release point. The bombardier flipped the switch and ten 500-pound bombs raced for the railroad station four miles below.

Then the explosions from the antiaircraft fire were every-where. It was all about them in every direction, as if they had flown into a violent, dark storm. Then came a thundering crash, with fragments of flak piercing the thin skin of the aircraft. The plane bounced and rocked violently from the concussion.

Rang, in the nose of the plane, was sure that it would go into a spin. He did not wait for the pilot to sound the bail-out alarm. With his parachute on, he dove out of the ship and into the fierce barrage of enemy fire. Others who bailed out at that moment were Lt James A. Thompson and Sgt Ludwig Verboys.

The blast of antiaircraft fire had severed the hydraulic line, knocked out the number four engine, and torn the elevator cable. Even with all of that damage, however, aircraft commander Frank W. Ellis was able to nurse the plane to an emergency landing on the island of Malta, 45 miles away.

The official memorandum of the Casualty Branch of the US Army, dated 19 July 1944, reads in part as follows:

> Any possibility that the subject personnel are still alive seems very remote when it is considered that at the time they bailed out they were in the midst of a heavy barrage of flak, that they were probably over water since the aircraft was on a 45 degree course over the target which would immediately carry it northeast of the target over the Strait of Messina, that they have not been reported as prisoners of war or internees, that they have not returned to duty and that twelve months have elapsed since their disappearance during which time no word has been received from them and no information has been received from any source indicating that they are alive.
>
> In view of the foregoing facts and circumstances, it is concluded that three persons considered herein may not reasonably be presumed to be living within the meaning of Section 5, Public Law 490, 7 March 1942, as amended.[1]

It was as if the black bursts of antiaircraft fire had consumed Bernard Rang and his two fellow crew members. There was no opportunity to search for them because the enemy controlled the land, sea, and air in the vicinity. All that remained to be done was to notify the next of kin that their boys would not be coming home.

Notes

1. War Department, Headquarters Army Air Forces, *Missing Air Crew Report*, AG 704, 15 July 1944.

Corregidor

We (Whitcomb, Renka, and Dey) took shelter in the ruins of an old stone building as bombs from the high-flying planes pounded Malinta Hill, about 100 yards to the southeast of us.* We felt the shock waves from each exploding bomb. As soon as the raid was over, all of us from the boat raced through the rubble to the western entrance to Malinta Tunnel. A warm feeling of security came over me the moment we entered the big arch of the tunnel.

Malinta Tunnel was 1,400 feet long and 30 feet wide. From where we stood, we could not see the other end. It seemed gigantic. We saw officers and men who were casual and relaxed, and dressed in freshly washed uniforms. They were not like the shaggy, haggard men we had left back in the field on Bataan. It seemed that we were in a different world, a secure place where life would be more peaceable.

We found an officer and explained that we were aircrew members and that we had just arrived from Bataan. He quickly put us in touch with an Air Corps colonel by the name of Newman R. Laughinghouse.

The colonel greeted us warmly and explained that we would be taken to Australia by submarine very soon. He carefully took our names in a notebook he carried:

> John Ivan Renka, Pilot
> Edgar D. Whitcomb, Navigator
> James Dey, Bombardier

Aircrew members were needed in Australia as more and more new bombers arrived from the United States. Getting our names in the colonel's book seemed to make it official. Soon we would be on our way back to our bombardment group in Australia. What a break for us!

---

*Continued from Chapter 12, "War Plan Orange III."

We had taken a big gamble in leaving the area at kilometer 182, where the surrender was taking place. We could have been shot at any moment by the hoards of Japanese soldiers who came streaming over the hills. We could have been strafed by enemy planes as we made our way across the seven miles from Mariveles to Corregidor. The high-flying bombers that arrived at Corregidor at the same time we arrived could have snuffed us out had their bombardiers made a slightly different setting on their bombsights. None of those things had happened. We had gambled and we had won. We were overjoyed at the prospect of soon being back with the guys in the 19th Bombardment Group. It seemed like a dream come true. It had been more than three months since I (Ed Whitcomb) had seen an American bomber. I was ready to go to Australia.

"Now, while we are waiting for the arrival of the submarine, you will be assigned to the 4th Marine Regiment on beach defense," the colonel explained. That seemed reasonable enough. We would not have to be in the tunnel while we were waiting for our transportation.

The next morning I was having breakfast with a group of husky marine officers, outdoors on the south side of Malinta Hill. Col Samuel L. Howard was there with some of his high-ranking officers. I was amazed that they did not run for cover when a barrage of artillery fire erupted from the Bataan shore. Being on the south side of the hill, they apparently felt secure. I did not.

After the breakfast my new commander, Capt Austin Shofner, escorted me to the eastern end of the island and explained that I would be in charge of an artillery piece. It was said to be a British 75. I had heard of French 75s before, but never a British 75. Under my command was a young Filipino 3d lieutenant, a graduate of the Philippine Military Academy.[1] After we became acquainted, I learned that the crew of five Filipinos were very familiar with the gun. Upon my command, they would load and aim the gun and do everything but fire it. We seemed to enjoy a good relationship as I used every possible means to avoid letting my command know that I knew absolutely nothing about the weapon. I was helped in this by the fact that we were under siege from artillery fire and from bombing and strafing airplanes from the first moment.

Renka and Dey had assignments on other parts of the island and I had no occasion to see them. In their place another old friend appeared. As I looked down the road near my gun position, I was surprised to see Dayton L. Drachenberg. A native of Rosenberg, Texas, he was a photographic officer from the 19th Group. We had been close friends from the time we had arrived at Clark Field six months before. After that, we had been together at Cabcaben Field on Bataan for three months. It was good to have someone from the bombardment group to visit with. The only time I had an opportunity to visit with anyone other than the Filipino gun crew was when the chow truck came around at about 11 o'clock at night. Some of the marines from nearby gun positions would then congregate for a visit while we ate. We also met at the same place at dawn, when a Navy corpsman boiled some pretty terrible coffee in a pan over an open fire.

We were frequently entertained by a family of monkeys that came in the mornings begging for crusts of bread. We assumed that they were longtime residents of the area since our location was known as Monkey Point.

The Japanese set up more than 100 artillery pieces on Bataan, two and one-half miles across the channel to the north. Artillery attacks and aerial bombing raids were a way of life from that first day at Monkey Point.

During lulls in the bombing and shelling, Drachenberg and I were able to salvage a number of useful items from the debris where officers' quarters once stood. We found a footlocker, an innerspring mattress, a can of Kentucky Club tobacco, a pipe, a silver spoon, and a number of other useful items. We dragged the mattress to a spot near our gun position, then dug deep trenches on each side so that at the first sound of artillery fire we could roll into the trenches for protection from the hours of shelling which would follow.

Artillery barrages were so frequent and intense that the area all about us was sprinkled with jagged pieces of steel shrapnel. Within a few days the footlocker located about 20 feet from our trenches took a direct hit. My can of Kentucky Club tobacco, the pipe, and other treasures were blown to smithereens so that not a shred of any item was salvageable.

One of the delightful features of Corregidor was that it was free from the mosquitoes that had plagued us all through those miserable months in the jungles of Bataan. Another good feature of our new home was that we could slip over to the south side of the island, where it was relatively safe from the shelling and bombing, for a cool refreshing swim.

After little more than a week on Corregidor, we were heartened by radio news that American planes had bombed Tokyo, Japan. I had no idea that two members of Charlie Lunn's first class were navigating those planes. Our spirits were raised and we began to believe that maybe the Americans had at last gained the offensive. Maybe reinforcements would be coming so that we could defend Corregidor.

There was never any word of a submarine to take us off the island, though we waited patiently. There was no doubt in anyone's mind that a Japanese invasion of the island was imminent as the bombing and shelling became more and more intense. It was especially severe on 2 May, after I had been on Corregidor for three weeks. Gen Jonathan Wainwright later wrote that the Japanese had hit Corregidor with 1,800,000 pounds of artillery shells on that date. It was estimated that the 240-mm howitzers delivered 12 shells a minute onto the tiny island. In addition, there had been 13 air raids that day. Two days later, Corregidor was hit by 16,000 shells in twenty-four hours. We survived it all, with no idea that the Japanese were targeting our sector for a planned landing on the island. My one hope was that I would hear from Colonel Laughing-house before the invasion came.

On the night of 5 May at about 11:00, there was an unusual amount of firing to the north of my position. As it became more and more intense, we became aware that the moment had come. Dark streaks of clouds blotted out the moon, presenting a sinister atmosphere. The artillery fire stopped as abruptly as it had begun. Then came the chatter of machine-gun and small-arms fire.

Drachenberg was away at his duty station and I was alone with my Filipino gun crew. From the flares and the flashes I saw, it was apparent that the Japanese were landing on the north shore of the island about 400 yards from my gun position. There was nothing we could do but wait. Our gun was mounted on a

108

semicircular track and pointed in a southeasterly direction. There was no way that we could participate in the battle unless the Japanese swept around the eastern tip of Corregidor.

We waited throughout the night, with gunfire all about us. Then, at first light of the new day, we disengaged the breech-block from the gun and threw it over the cliff so that it would not be available to the enemy. After that, we moved to a position on a ridge to the northwest of the Navy communications tunnel. There I joined Drachenberg and others in forming a defense position along the ridge.

History tells that Monkey Point was overrun by the Japanese as of 0100 on 6 May. It seems to disregard the stalwart crew of an antiquated British 75 field gun that held out until dawn on that date. According to the historical account, we were behind the enemy lines from 0100 until dawn.

We moved to a point near Denver Hill and organized a line of riflemen on the ridge. A .30-caliber machine gun next to me was firing in the direction of the oncoming enemy until a sniper drilled the machine-gun operator through the upper right arm. Another shot put the gun out of commission. We were unable to tell where the shot came from. It may have come from a sniper somewhere behind a tree stump. We never learned where.

As Drachenberg and I, and a couple of other officers, were in a huddle trying to establish some strategy, a mortar shell landed between us. Drachenberg and the other two fell. Drachenberg had a hole the size of a silver dollar in the top of his steel helmet, and blood was running down his face.

I ran down the hill to the Navy tunnel and procured a couple of stretchers along with some people to help move the injured men to the tunnel. It turned out that Drachenberg's serious injury was shrapnel in the intestines. The wound to his head was only superficial. One of the other wounded officers later died.

The real tragedy was that it all happened about an hour before Gen Jonathan Wainwright and his party rode east from Malinta Tunnel to Denver Hill in a Chevrolet automobile to meet with the Japanese and surrender. Before that trip, the general had sent a radio message to the president of the United States. It read in part:

> With broken heart and head bowed in sadness but not in shame I report . . . that today I must arrange terms for the surrender of the fortified islands of Manila Bay. . . . Please say to the nation that my troops and I have accomplished all that is humanly possible and that we have upheld the best traditions of the United States and its army. . . . With profound regret and with continued pride in my gallant troops, I go to meet the Japanese commander.[2]

Five long months after the Japanese had dropped their bombs on Clark Field, we became prisoners of war. It seemed as if all sense of emotion had been drained from my body by the events of the past days, weeks, and months. I was no longer afraid. There was no reason to be afraid. Nothing could happen that was worse than what we had endured. We were helpless and it seemed that all hope was gone.

The Japanese soldiers ordered a couple hundred of us to form in a column of fours. We then marched to the north a couple hundred yards to the Corregidor airstrip known as Kindley Field. Somewhere along the way, the Japanese halted our column and searched each of us. Watches, fountain pens, wallets, bracelets—all things of value—were extracted from us by Japanese soldiers.

From Kindley Field we were marched westward past the middle of the island known as Middle Sides. We had no idea where we were going. At some point we turned around and headed back toward the east. It was growing dark when we finally halted. At that moment we were located on a section of the old Corregidor electric rail line. We were ordered to sit down. Then we were ordered to sleep. Sleep? How could we sleep? We were in such a close formation that when we lay back we were each lying on the legs of the person behind us.

We had not eaten food of any kind for more than 48 hours because the invasion of the island had come at our mealtime the night before. No food was offered to us. That was of no concern because there was no feeling of hunger. There was little feeling of any kind. All hopes were gone for getting a submarine back to Australia. All hopes were gone for getting back to my outfit. All that remained was the vague possibility that there might be an exchange of prisoners or that the American forces would retake the Philippines. No one dreamed that it would be more than three years before the American forces would return to the Philippines to free the prisoners.

Notes

1. Newly commissioned officers in the Philippine Army served in the grade of 3d lieutenant. Ricardo T. Jose, *The Philippine Army* (Manila: Ateneo de Manila University Press, 1992), 57–63.

2. Gen Jonathan Wainwright to President Roosevelt, radio message, subject: Surrender of Manila Bay, 6 May 1942 in Jonathan M. Wainwright, *General Wainwright's Story* (Garden City, N.Y.: Doubleday & Co., 1946), 122–23.

William Scott Warner

When Bataan fell Scott Warner, along with classmates Jay Horowitz and Jack Jones, were destined to take part in the most infamous event of the entire war in the Pacific—the Bataan Death March. It was a gruesome march for 12,000 American and 68,000 Filipino soldiers. Thousands died as Allied troops were herded along the 60 miles of grimy, dusty road from Mariveles on the southern tip of Bataan to San Fernando in central Luzon.[1]

Scott Warner's plane survived the first day of the war. His B-17 was one of the lucky ones which had been moved to Del Monte Field, Mindanao, the day before the initial Japanese raid on Clark Field. The day after the war started, Scott had navigated a bombing mission from Mindanao, dropping 100-pound bombs on Japanese shipping north of Luzon. From there, he had flown to Lingayen Gulf to attack a Japanese landing force. Being low on fuel, Scott's plane landed at Clark Field for the night. Early the next morning the pilot, fearful of being caught by an early morning raid, panicked and quickly gathered a crew to fly back to Del Monte. Scott Warner was left behind at Clark Field, and his B-17 never returned. He waited for his opportunity to fly again, but it never came.

Scott busied himself with various duties. Three weeks later, he was headed south on a railroad car that was loaded with field rations and ammunition. Clark Field was being evacuated. The cargo was bound for Bataan. At San Fernando he was with Jack Jones and others, frantically unloading the train's cargo. At this point, he became weak and lost consciousness from an attack of dengue fever. About a week later, he revived and learned that he was in a field hospital somewhere on Bataan. When he was able to travel, he was transferred to the airstrip at Cabcaben where I was located. From there he was ordered to Quinauan Point on the west coast, assigned as an artillery spotter. From Quinauan Point, he was able to observe Japanese warships entering and leaving Subic Bay. Scott directed artillery fire for two ancient French 75s and one three-inch naval gun. The American and Filipino forces doggedly held the line against the Japanese for more than three months. Ultimately, however, the Japanese were able to break through. Orders came down for Scott to withdraw to Mariveles Harbor for surrender to the Japanese. He obeyed his commander and joined hundreds of bewildered men huddled in groups at Mariveles Harbor while Japanese officers tried to determine the next action.

The Japanese officer in charge seemed to be without orders as to what to do with the captured Allied forces. Consequently, the prisoners languished for two days on the dirt airstrip in sweltering sun. No food of any kind was provided. Fortunately, Capt Ed Dyess, commander of the 21st Pursuit Squadron, was permitted to distribute some C rations to the beleaguered prisoners.

Finally the Japanese commander ordered the prisoners to march, but many of the soldiers were too weak from disease and starvation to walk very far. Some tried to assist their buddies, but were too weak. They fell. Many were bayoneted or bashed in the head with rifle butts and left along the road to die. At rest stops they were searched and relieved of whatever valuable possessions they had been able to save through the ordeal of the past four months. Removal of each personal item from the prisoners extracted memories from another world that seemed far, far away. High school or college class rings, silver bracelets given by loved ones, watches, money—everything of value—were taken. Nothing escaped the eager, searching fingers of their Japanese captors, but items of their personal property would be of no use to many of the prisoners anyway. Too many of them would perish on the 60-mile Bataan Death March.

The prisoners finally reached Cabcaben Field, where the Japanese had installed artillery to fire on the island of Corregidor three miles across the water. The horrified prisoners were placed in front of the Japanese artillery pieces, a move designed to discourage return fire from the American guns on Corregidor. However, the American prisoners bolted and ran when the firing started. The Japanese made no effort to bring them back at that time, but later rounded them up and continued marching toward San Fernando.

As he marched, Scott saw prisoners crazed with thirst being bayoneted by the Japanese guards for breaking out of line to get a drink of water. A continuous display of dead soldiers marked the roadside along the route.

At one point Scott was herded into a barbed wire enclosure with a group of about 200 other prisoners. They were so crowded that there was not room to lie down. At least a dozen dead and decaying bodies were in the area when they arrived, and there were more when the prisoners moved on two days later.

After nine days of marching, Scott was given a handful of cooked, dry rice. That was the first morsel of food he had received for nine days of marching in the torrid Philippine sun. He was physically exhausted, sustained only by an indomitable spirit and will to live. Others, healthier than Scott, died because they gave up hope. Giving up was not an option for a rugged boy from Virginia's Appalachian Mountains.

When the exhausted prisoners staggered into San Fernando, they were packed into sweltering hot boxcars so tightly that they could hardly move. They endured those sweltering conditions while being transported to Camp O'Donnell. It would be their new home for the following two months. After leaving the train, they sat in rows on the ground to be addressed by an arrogant, one-armed Japanese captain. He stood on a box and addressed his weary audience through an interpreter. His message was short and to the point: "You are our eternal enemy! You may win this one, but there will be another."

Camp O'Donnell was ill prepared to handle the 7,000 starving men. There were bamboo slats for bunks. Long lines of thirsty men stood for hours at a single spigot waiting for drinking water. The death rate continued to mount until there were as many as 100 deaths in a single day. Filipinos were encamped across the road in another area. Their death rate was even higher, reaching 300 to 400 in a single day!

The prisoners thought it was good news when, after a couple of months, they learned that they would be moving by truck to a place called Cabanatuan in the central part of Luzon. Scott always had the thought that a new location would be less torturous. It was hard to imagine that it could be any worse than Camp O'Donnell.

The housing at the new camp was a little better, but the death rate remained about the same. There was no good news, with one day being like the other in camp. Disease and death stalked the starving prisoners relentlessly. Scott suffered through attacks of malaria, beriberi, dengue fever, and pellagra with scant optimism for the future other than not to become another statistic on the list of those who had not survived.

Since there seemed to be so little hope under prevailing conditions, Scott volunteered for the first group to be moved to Japan. In November 1942, he was transported to Manila and loaded aboard an ancient ship named *Nagato Maru.* The crowded hold was a mass of stinking humanity. The old vessel became a new place of torture. Through weary eyes Scott observed the nameplate which told him that the ship had been built in Hong Kong in 1914. He also observed that his body was quickly covered with lice. There was no relief from them, no change of clothes—only the misery of the ever-present insects crawling on his body and in his hair.

The transport made a stop at Takao, on the Island of Formosa, where Chinese coolies refueled the ship's coal bunkers by bringing baskets of coal two at a time with one on each end of a bamboo pole balanced on their shoulders. After being resupplied, the ship continued its journey to Japan, arriving on Thanksgiving Day. The prisoners were first lodged in barracks at Osaka; then, two months later, all officers were moved to Zentsuji Prisoner of War Camp.

The November weather was cold in Japan. The prisoners welcomed news that winter uniforms were being furnished. The khaki uniforms, which had been worn on the death march, at Camp O'Donnell, at Cabanatuan, and on the ship to Japan, were threadbare, dirty, and full of body lice. In addition to the British winter uniforms, which had been brought by the Japanese from Singapore, the weary prisoners were afforded their first hot bath in more than six months. Old uniforms were burned and, at last, the men were rid of the pesky lice that had been their constant companions for more than two months.

Scott had seen Jay Horowitz from time to time in the Cabanatuan Prison Camp, but he had not seen Jack Jones

116

since they had left Cabcaben Field. He never saw any of his classmates again.

Scott's parents, back in Richlands, Virginia, had received no word from him for a year and a half, other than a notice from the War Department dated 9 April 1943, that their son was missing in action. That message had stated, in part:

> The records of the War Department show your son, William Scott Warner, O-409909, Air Corps, missing in action in the Philippine Islands since April 9, 1942. I fully appreciate your concern and deep interest. You will, without further request on your part, receive immediate notification of any change in your son's status. That the far-flung operations of the present war, the ebb and flow of combat over great distances in isolated areas, and the characteristics of our enemies have imposed upon some of us this heavy burden of uncertainty with respect to the safety of our loved ones is deeply regretted.[2]

> Nothing further had been received from the War Department. Scott's father went to his work regularly as a coal wharfman, filling coal tenders on locomotives for the local railroad. Early each morning, he would be seen hurrying to the post office to see if there were any further word about his son.

There was nothing more from the government, but one day just before the Christmas holidays of 1943, Scott's father received a small package in the mail postmarked from Australia. It contained a letter and a plastic phonograph record. From the letter, John Warner learned that the writer had heard Scott's voice on Radio Tokyo. He hurried home with the phonograph record, where he and his wife, Rebecca, heard their son's voice for the first time in more than three years. They were sure that it was his voice. There could be no mistake about that. They listened intently as they heard:

> Anyone hearing this: This is Lt William Scott Warner, U.S. Army Air Corps, speaking from Zentsuji, POW Camp, Shikoku Island, Japan, to my parents, Mr and Mrs John H. Warner of Richlands, Virginia, U.S.A.

> I have been in Japan for almost a year. I am well. I have had no mail from you since leaving the States. Very anxious to hear from you all or anyone. Hope you are enjoying good health. I hope that I will be with you soon. Tell Joe, Dot, Ken and Bob hello.

> I am sending my love to all and I wish you a Merry Christmas and a Happy New Year!
>
> This is Lt William Scott Warner speaking to my parents, Mr and Mrs John H. Warner of Richlands, Virginia, U.S.A.[3]

It all seemed unreal to his parents, who had waited so hopefully for so many months. They played the record over and over again.

They were finally convinced that it was true as more and more letters from Australia, New Zealand, and various islands in the Pacific poured into the little post office at Richlands. Many letters contained plastic phonograph records, but others simply reported that they had heard Warner's message: He wanted his parents notified that he was a prisoner and that he was safe.

Scott Warner remained a prisoner of war in Japan two more years, until war's end. He had flown a single combat mission in the war. He had spotted artillery fire against shipping at Subic Bay in a hopeless effort to stop the advance of the Japanese. He had survived the horrible Bataan Death March, and he had spent three years and four months as a prisoner of war under conditions more horrible than he could ever have imagined. But at war's end, he returned safely to his family and loved ones in Richlands, Virginia.

Notes

1. There are no precise statistics concerning the number of men forced to participate in the Bataan Death March, only "educated guesses" as one historian puts it. The same source estimates that of 65,000 to 70,000 Filipino participants, as many as 10,000 may have perished. It is believed that 10,000 to 12,000 American prisoners began the horrendous 60-mile trek. About 650 are thought to have died before reaching San Fernando. See Stanley L. Falk, *Bataan: March of Death* (New York: W. W. Norton, 1962), 196–98.

2. War Department, "Missing in Action Message," 9 April 1943, copy of message provided to author by William S. Warner in 1990.

3. Information provided by William S. Warner to author, 1990.

Jay M. Horowitz

Jay Horowitz and I (Ed Whitcomb) had been at Clark Field together on that day in December 1941 when a mighty armada of Japanese bombers crushed the United States forces. We were not together at the time of the surrender of the Philippines and I never saw him again.

Jay Horowitz's time as a prisoner had grown into 32 months.* He felt fortunate when he learned that he was one of a group that was being moved from the miserable Cabanatuan Prison Camp to Bilibid Prison in Manila. Everyone knew that they would be shipped from there to Japan or Manchuria. It would be good to get away from the hot tropical climate of the Philippines, away from the flies and mosquitoes and away from the camp where he had seen so many of his fellow prisoners die.

After just a few days at Bilibid Prison, 1,169 ragged and emaciated American prisoners were marched through the streets of Manila to the dock area of Manila Bay. Filipinos along the streets looked on them with pity. By now, the local people were used to the sight because they had seen thousands upon thousands of Americans in the same condition marching to and from the Bilibid Prison. Long ago they had learned of the severe penalty for trying to provide food, water, or even a word of encouragement to the American soldiers.

It was about 11:00 A.M., 13 December 1944, when the prisoners reached Pier No. 7. It was known as the "Million Dollar Pier" because it was reputed to be one of the finest piers in the world at that time. The *Oryoku Maru*, a 15,000-ton Japanese cabin-type vessel was waiting to be loaded (figures 1 and 2). It was a fine-looking craft, having been designed for luxury travel in the Orient before the war. To the waiting prisoners, it looked like a welcome change from the life they had endured for the past months in the crowded, stinking prison camp.

---

*Information in this chapter comes from Gen Austin Montgomery's personal papers held in Alexandria, Virginia.

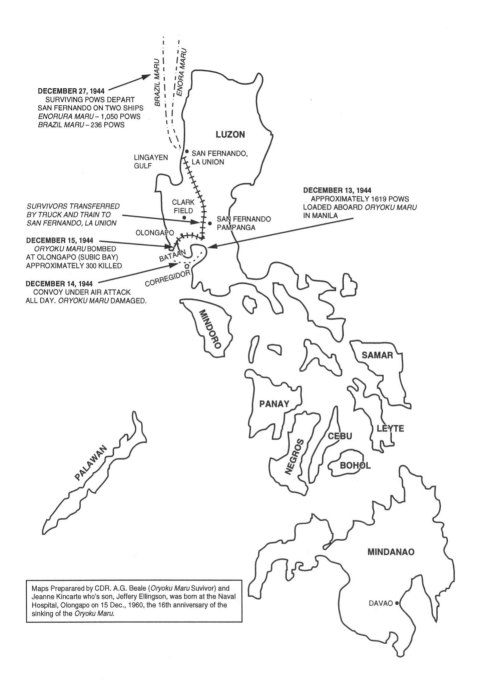

Figure 1. Route of Horowitz POW Ship

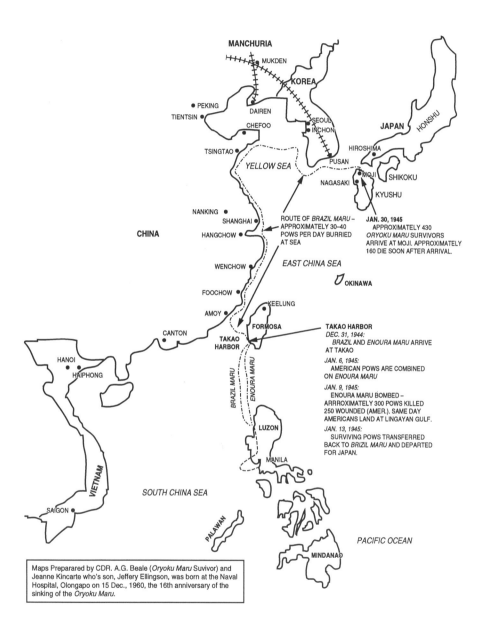

Figure 2. Route of Horowitz POW Ship (Greater Range)

Across the wide Manila Bay, they could see the island of Corregidor and the peninsula of Bataan. Nobody wanted to think of the days they had spent there or of the Bataan Death March. At long last, after four hours in the scorching Manila sun, the prisoners boarded the *Oryoku Maru*. Unfortunately for them, 1,500 Japanese civilians occupied the luxury cabins on the top decks of the ship. The Americans found their quarters in the three cargo holds 20 feet below the top deck.

The men were so crowded that Colonel Beecher complained to the Japanese interpreter, "The conditions in this hold are so crowded that men are fainting—you must move some of the men out. There is not enough air in here."[1]

"There will be 200 more men brought into this hold. You will make room for them" came the reply from Mr Wada, the arrogant interpreter.

The Japanese soldiers pushed the prisoners down the ladder striking them with rifle butts. Men were knocked down and off the ladder, falling on the grumbling men below. In the lower bays, unable to stand erect, they were forced to assume a crouching position because of the height of the ceilings. About 45 men were crammed into each bay.

After more than six terrifying hours in the stifling, steaming quarters, Colonel Beecher again appealed for help. "For God's sake, Mr Wada, give us some water. The men are drinking their urine."

"You will get no more water, and stop making so much noise," snarled Wada.

Not only was there no water but there were no toilet facilities available for the 1,619 men in the three holds. Finally, four buckets with a capacity of seven and one-half gallons each were lowered into the holds and placed in one corner. Within a couple of hours, they were full to overflowing.

The temperature in the hold stood at between 100° and 110°. There was no breeze and there was no circulation of air. The men screamed and complained so loudly that, at about two o'clock in the morning, the hatches were completely battened down, cutting off all air except that which seeped in around the hatch covers. The temperature was then estimated to be at 120°. During the time before the hatch was opened at four o'clock, the air became even more foul and at least 100 men passed out.

Men became deranged in the black of the night, screaming for water and air. Some would lash out with their fists or feet at the person crowded next to them. One screamed, "He's trying to murder me. He is slashing me with a knife."

At about 3:00 A.M. the *Oryoku Maru* weighed anchor and headed west across Manila Bay toward the China Sea. The light of day exposed misery and death, and a quietness of resignation fell over the ship. Suddenly an explosion from one of the guns on the top deck shattered the spell. Then the drone of airplane engines paralyzed those who still had feelings. The *Oryoku Maru* was being strafed by machine gun fire and bullets were ricocheting into the holds.

An American officer edged his way to the top of the hold and gave a blow-by-blow description of what was happening. American planes on the first pass at the ship had wiped out the gun crew above the hatch.

The attack on the ship lasted until four o'clock in the afternoon when it became apparent that the *Oryoku Maru* had been badly damaged. The firing of guns had a sobering effect on all of the men. After the raid subsided, men again wailed and cried for water and air. Several of the prisoners had been hit by ricocheting bullets, but Horowitz was uninjured, though starved for food and water.

At 8:00 P.M. the Japanese took American medical personnel from the hold to treat Japanese civilians who had been injured. One American medical officer reported that hundreds of the Japanese civilians had been killed or wounded. After the medics rendered first aid to the injured Japanese, the soldiers beat them. The medical officer said it was because, "our planes were sinking their ships and killing Japanese, including civilians."

While the doctors were attending the Japanese, they made repeated requests to the guards for food and water for the prisoners in the holds. The Japanese in charge replied with a series of screams, "We will do nothing for you."

The medical officers determined that conditions in the forward hold were even worse than midship. There, the prisoners were so crowded that it was difficult to determine the exact number of men who were unconscious or dead from suffocation.

During the second night at sea, conditions in the holds continued to deteriorate with much screaming and moaning. The suffering from thirst was so acute that many men went out of their minds.

"Get him! Get him! He's got a knife!" was heard again in the darkness of the night through the wailing and moaning.

The senior American officer again transmitted the message to the Japanese guards that the men were drinking their urine due to intense dehydration. There was no response whatsoever.

As the blackness of the night melted into grotesque forms of men lying one against another in the stinking, filthy hold, muffled conversations and moaning could be heard throughout the entire area. Then came the sound of a motor launch pulling alongside. From the noise on the top deck, it soon became apparent that the Japanese civilians were being evacuated from the damaged ship.

At about 8:30 A.M. the Japanese in charge announced through the hatch opening that the prisoners would be evacuated from the ship to the Olongapo Naval Reservation on Subic Bay. They were informed that they were not to take their shoes or any other gear as they would have to swim 300 yards to shore. Then they were told that the Japanese guards had been instructed to "shoot to kill" if anyone got out of line.

Before any prisoners left the ship, American planes came over again and dealt more damage to the ship. About 45 minutes after the raid, the prisoners were ordered to evacuate the ship by jumping over the side and swimming to shore.

When the order was given to come out of the hold and climb the ladder up to the deck, Horowitz was greatly relieved. He was numb from the ordeal of the past couple of days. Prospects for getting fresh air and getting off the ship alive had given him new energy as he climbed the ladder onto the deck. It would be good to get back on solid ground again.

Horowitz was in a dazed condition as he pulled the weight of his frail body up the ladder to the top deck. As he reached the top deck, a fresh breeze swept across the ship. For a moment, the brightness of the day blinded him. Then he saw Subic Bay, the palm trees along the shore, and the mountains to the east.

He also saw the wretched men about him removing their shoes and jumping off the deck into the clear blue water of Subic Bay some 20 feet below.

He left the ship and felt a dull shock as his body splashed into the cool water along with the mass of humanity flailing and endeavoring to swim to the distant shore. His once strong body was so weak that it was difficult to make it to the shore. Fellow prisoners who could not swim were clinging to boards that had been thrown from the ship.

He put more and more distance between himself and the *Oryoku Maru*. Suddenly, there was the rat-tat-tat of machine-gun fire from the shore. Japanese soldiers on the shore fired on and killed several officers making their way to shore on a raft.

There was no way out. There was nothing to do but swim and pray. Swimming in his shirt and trousers was so much more difficult than when he used to swim at Miami Beach. However, that was another world—a world he might never see again.

Then came a sound that he had learned instinctively to fear. Over the noise of the swimmers shouting, he heard the drone of airplane engines in the distance. In a moment he saw them—a flight of American Navy planes bearing in on the *Oryoku Maru*. When they strafed the ship or dropped bombs, they were certain to kill many Americans. For those in the water, it was as if they were watching a tragic scene in a movie. They were frozen in fear with the reality of their plight. There was nothing they could do but swim and watch and wait to hear the shattering machine-gun fire and the scream of falling bombs. It was certain to be a quick ending for many of the hundreds of prisoners who had clung for hours to a thin thread of hope for survival.

Then came the miracle of miracles. Just prior to the bomb release point, the lead plane, without firing or dropping bombs, pulled up and wagged his wings in recognition. The other planes followed. The swimmers had been saved. An astute flight leader had recognized the white skin of the swimmers and had led his flight off to another target. The hundreds of swimmers would never know the identity of the American flyer who spared them on that day in December 1944. To most of them it would never make any difference.

Those who survived the Japanese machine-gun fire finally reached the Olongapo shore. Some of the survivors fell upon the ground exhausted, others sloshed and milled about the area, trying to find a missing buddy or join up with friends they had known before. All were barefooted and unshaven. Many wore only short trousers and a shirt.

The thirsty men soon found a pipe of fresh drinking water and quickly formed a line. Some enjoyed the first drink of fresh water since they had left Manila two days before. Soon the Japanese in charge were herding them into a tennis court area that was surrounded with woven chicken wire. The enclosure was not large enough to hold all of the men comfortably.

Several attempts were made to take a roll call of the prisoners who had survived the trip. After several attempts, it was determined that of the 1,619 prisoners who had sailed from Manila's Million Dollar Pier on 13 December 1944, less than 1,300 had survived. More than 300 helpless American prisoners of war had died in a 38-hour period from suffocation, starvation, drowning, and cold-blooded murder.

The hard cement of the tennis court was uncomfortable and there was no protection from the glare and heat of the sun. Such conditions only added to the already dazed condition of the weary prisoners. Good news came when the senior Japanese officer announced that there would be a cooked meal that evening. The news quickly spread throughout the group. Conditions were looking better for the prisoners. Perhaps the worst of it was over and things would be better from then on. With high hopes for a decent meal, the starved prisoners watched the big red ball of the afternoon sun sink into the China Sea. Twilight faded into darkness, but no food of any kind was served to the weary prisoners.

In the darkness, as the cool breezes of night swept across the shore, the scantly clad men suffered from the cold, with only their skinny bodies crowded one to another to provide warmth. Darkness brought out a cover of bright stars in the heavens above. At first, the planets were visible; then there were the stars, which Horowitz knew so well—Deneb, Vega, and Arcturus had helped him guide his mighty Flying Fortress across the wide Pacific so many moons ago.

The stars did not look like they had looked from the roof of the old San Sebastian Hotel in Coral Gables, where Charlie Lunn had so patiently identified them for the cadets. It had been exciting then, but from the tennis court at Olongapo on that December night in 1944, the stars looked different. They had little relevance to anything other than to tell Horowitz by their apparent movement how much of the miserable night had passed.

The following day on the tennis court (December 16th) was a replay of the day before—boiling hot sun, hard cement, and no food.

Late in the evening of the third day (December 17th), the Japanese delivered one sack of uncooked rice for the 1,300 men on the tennis court. By that time it was too dark to distribute the food, so it was not dispensed to the men until the next morning. Each person's share was one heaping teaspoon and one level teaspoon of the hard rice kernels. No other food was provided. The ration was the same on each of the next three days.

The prisoners spent five days and six nights on the tennis court. Then the Japanese loaded them onto trucks and hauled them across Zig-Zag Pass to San Fernando. After a couple of days there in the jail and jail yard, they were loaded on a train, 120 men to a boxcar—so crowded that there was insufficient fresh air. Again there were no sanitary facilities provided for them. The trip ended 18 hours later at San Fernando La Union, a port on the China Sea about 150 miles to the north of San Fernando. By then it was Christmas Day of 1944. It was Jay's third Christmas in captivity. Christmas dinner consisted of one rice ball mixed with compotes. The next day (December 26th) the ration was the same, no more no less.

At about eight o'clock on the morning of 27 December, the prisoners embarked on two different ships, the *Brazil Maru* and the *Enoura Maru*. The two then joined a convoy which the prisoners learned was headed for Takao, Formosa (later Taiwan). They arrived on 2 January 1945 after six more days of starvation on the hell ships.

At that point, all prisoners moved to the hold of the *Enoura Maru*. Horses and men had been quartered there before and the area had not been cleaned. It was filled with a mass of manure, urine, and flies. There they remained for one restless week, until 9 January when the monotony of their routine was interrupted. Again, they heard the excruciating drone of aircraft engines. There was antiaircraft fire and then again the whistle of bombs. The *Enoura Maru* rocked violently from near misses as the prisoners huddled, breathlessly waiting for the next attack. They were like caged animals in the holds of the ship. Steel fragments from the bombs whizzed in, killing between 350 and 400 men and injuring many more. There was no escape from the death, the mangled bodies, the screaming, and the agony. There was no aid, no medicine, and no bandages except undershirts and dirty towels.

There was no assistance of any kind from the Japanese for three days after the bombing. Then there was help, but only for those with minor injuries. For the seriously injured, there was nothing but death. Dead bodies were stacked like cord wood in the center of the hatch area. The place was described as looking like a human butcher shop with blood, guts, and dead bodies. The injured and dying moaned in agony for three days and nights.

Three days after the raid by the American planes, the Japanese appeared and started the grizzly process of removing the dead bodies from the *Enoura Maru*. A cargo sling was used to lift as many as 20 of the bodies out of the hold at a time. Others were removed by tying ropes about arms, legs, or torso, as if they were dead animals being hauled away. Though there was a certain sameness about their appearance, some of them were recognizable. Jay had made the Bataan Death March with them. They had suffered two and one-half years of prison camp at Cabanatuan together. They had endured the bombing and strafing of the *Oryoku Maru* together, and then the torture of being cooped up in the tennis court at Subic Bay together.

There had been rumors of all kinds: that there would be a prisoner exchange, that there had been an American landing in the Philippines, and all manner of things. Still, each new rumor had been embraced with the same enthusiasm as on the first day they had been taken prisoner. The rumors were the substance of the hope that kept the wretched souls alive. Now, their one hope was that when they reached Japan they would have better food and better living conditions until the end of the war.

The last of the dead bodies were removed and stacked on the dock alongside the ship. Then the survivors were ordered to leave the hold of the *Enoura Maru* and to board the *Brazil Maru* for the trip to Japan.

The *Brazil Maru* departed the port of Takao, Formosa, for Japan on 13 January 1945, leaving the stack of human bodies on the dock to be cremated. It was one month to the day since 1,619 of them had departed from Manila's Million Dollar Pier. Almost half of their number had perished during those 31 days.

Away from Formosa, they should be out of the range of American planes. In a few days, they should arrive in Japan. No one knew what conditions would be like in their new camp, but of one thing they could be certain: It would be no worse than what they had experienced during the past three years as prisoners in the Philippines. Their new camp would be Moji on the island of Kyushu.

Jay never reached the Moji Prison Camp. After the *Brazil Maru* set sail for Japan in January, it encountered bitter winter weather. The soldiers' only clothing were shirts and trousers and such items as they were able to salvage from other prisoners who had died. Death was their constant companion as the *Brazil Maru* hugged the China coast on its trip northward toward Japan. The prisoners had been exposed to too much cruelty, too much starvation, and too much cold weather.

Austin Montgomery, a fellow prisoner, described it as follows:

> When first left Takao—Night of 13 January—about 15 died— some previously wounded—bodies were stacked in hospital area—first stripped of clothing by hospital corpsman under orders—salvageable clothing was then distributed to men in most need—Bodies were collected over a two-or three-day period before permission was obtained from Wada to get a burial detail to throw them overboard. First group of dead about 50—saw this on several occasions. . . . In the beginning the death rate was between 10 and 15 per day and got progressively worse—finally reaching a maximum of about 40 dead per day, a few days prior to arrival.

> When the prisoners died aboard the *Brazil Maru* they were stacked like wood and all of them presented a uniform appearance; lips were drawn back exposing teeth in a half

snarl due to skin contraction, ribs seemed to be bursting out of the bodies and where the stomach would be was a hollow, legs and arms were like pipe stems. A combination of cold and rigor mortis gave them a rigid, unreal appearance. The eyes were sunken. Most of them were stripped nude and all of them gave the definite appearance of starvation.[2]

On 23 January, when the interpreter called "roll out your dead," the body of Jay Horowitz was carried out onto the deck with the bodies of 39 other prisoners who had died during the night. A Navy corpsman under orders removed their clothing so it could be used by the survivors. Then their bodies were thrown overboard into the cold water of the East China Sea.

Notes

1. Gen Austin Montgomery, "His Diary," 1945, held in General Montgomery's Papers, Alexandria, Virginia.
2. Ibid.

The Super Fortresses

At our navigation school graduation exercise, Gen Davenport Johnson told us that if the US became involved in WWII, we must be able to reach out from our coastal frontiers to discover, locate, and destroy the enemy. November 1944 found four of our classmates far from our coastal frontiers.

Classmates Russell M. Vifquain, Jr., Berry P. Thompson, and Clarence R. Winter were on the tiny island of Saipan flying missions against the homeland of Japan, and Robert T. Arnoldus was flying missions out of Kharagpur, India. All were happy to be navigating on the B-29 Super Fortress, the world's finest and most powerful bomber.

Morale was high. America was on the offensive. The Yanks were well established on the continent of Europe on the way to Berlin, and MacArthur was back in the Philippines preparing to move on to Okinawa and Japan.

Robert Thermond Arnoldus had come to the Pan American Navigation School from Le Grande, Oregon, and upon graduation was assigned to Fort Douglas, Utah. Four November 1944 saw him flying from Kharagpur, India, on a B-29 Super Fortress of the Twentieth Air Force. Pilot of the big plane was Col Ted S. Faulkner who had been pilot for Louis G. Moslener, the first navigator lost in the attack on Pearl Harbor almost three years earlier. The target was to be the Japanese-held naval base at Singapore, but the big plane never reached the target. No one ever knew what happened to cause the trouble.

In the dark of night at 2030 hours another plane on the same mission received a radio message which said, "URGENT!" but no message followed. Then crew members of yet another plane saw a plane light up the sky with an explosion and fall into the sea at 11 degrees, 17 minutes north and 94 degrees, 44 minutes east. That was in the vicinity of the Andaman Islands in the Bay of Bengal. All other planes on the mission were accounted for, leaving little doubt that the exploding plane was the one being navigated by Major Arnoldus. An extensive search of the area by three land-base planes and one seaplane on the following day failed to locate any survivors. In addition to the navigator, 10 other crew members and one civilian war correspondent perished in the explosion.

Back on Saipan, the tiny island was crowded with big, silver Super Fortresses, which had been developed for the purpose of delivering bombs to Japan 1,500 miles to the north. Earlier, the Allies had attempted to bomb the island empire from the mainland of China. But all of the fuel for the planes in China had to be transported from India over the Burma Hump, which made it impossible to fly more than a few missions each month. To overcome that problem, the major portion of the B-29 operation had been concentrated in the Mariana Islands, consisting of Guam, Tinian, and Saipan. There, an abundance of fuel, equipment, and supplies could be transported from the United States by water with little interference from the enemy.

Russell M. ("Juny") Vifquain, Jr., had navigated his giant bomber to Saipan on 15 November 1944 and had flown his first bombing mission over Tokyo nine days later as a member of the XXI Bomber Command. It was the first time the capital city of Japan had been attacked from the air since his classmates, Harry McCool and Carl Wildner, had visited the city as members of the famous Doolittle Raid more than two and one-half years earlier.

This time it had been more than a nuisance raid—it was an attack by highly sophisticated aircraft loaded with tons of deadly explosives. Being without fighter protection, the crews had a great deal of uncertainty about what to expect from Japanese fighter planes and antiaircraft fire on the 3,000-mile mission.

The flight went according to schedule as the crews of 11 flyers headed north to Tokyo. Since it was their first mission to Japan, they were naturally anxious about the raid. They took the Japanese completely by surprise, however, and were not attacked by enemy planes as they approached their target. Nor were they damaged by antiaircraft fire. However, just before reaching the target, one engine on Vifquain's plane sputtered and died. Nevertheless, they dropped their bombs on their target. Five minutes later, a second engine failed. At the time, they were 1,500 miles from Saipan with no alternate fields available. In spite of repeated efforts by the pilot and crew chief, the engines refused to fire up again, leaving them in an exceedingly precarious situation.

With the plane losing altitude, pilots Col Samuel K. Harris and Lt Col George A. Shealy started preparing to ditch the plane when they were about 50 miles off the coast of Japan. Although they were almost certain to have to ditch the plane somewhere on the way to Saipan, the crew members laughed and joked as they chopped away at the interior of the big plane. Everything that would come loose was torn out and thrown overboard to lighten the plane. When the plane was about halfway to Saipan, the crew held a conference. They decided that they would ride the plane all the way home if it could be kept airborne. So, after strewing equipment and parts all of the way across the wide ocean from Japan to Saipan, the plane made an uneventful landing at their home base. It was the first time any B-29 had flown so far on two engines; consequently, the flight was given much publicity. According to a news release issued by the XXI Bomber Command Headquarters, the extremely accurate navigation by Vifquain was chiefly responsible for the ship's safe return to base.

The chief of the XXI Bomber Command was Maj Gen Curtis LeMay, a stocky, 39-year-old, cigar-chomping, serious-minded pilot who had wrought devastation on German cities with the mighty Eighth Air Force in Europe. Now he was in command of the mightiest force of heavy bombardment planes ever assembled.

LeMay soon learned that saturation bombing, as it had been employed in Europe, was not the most effective means of attacking Japan's mainland targets. Efforts at precision bombing were not accomplishing the desired results, even with the use of radar. The nature of targets was different in the Orient. In many cases, a factory would be merely the final assembly point for work that had been performed in hundreds of little home workshops clustered in the vicinity of the plant. Therefore, a new and awesome element that had not been much employed in Europe was used in the aerial warfare against the homeland of Japan. It was known as firebombing, and it seemed to be the only effective way to destroy the enemy's war potential.

Japanese cities were extremely vulnerable to fire. The great and venerable Adm Isoroku Yamamoto had said as early as 1939, "Cities being made of wood and paper would burn easily. The army talks big, but if war comes and there were large-scale air raids, there is no telling what would happen."

What did happen is one of the dark pages in the history of World War II. At the time, it was considered a matter of necessity to bring to a quick end a war which should not have happened against an enemy who had no plan but to win or die.

On 9 March 1945 Russell Vifquain was assigned to navigate one of 343 Super Fortresses of the XXI to employ this new tactic in bombing Tokyo from an altitude of 4,900 feet. It was his fourth raid from Saipan against the capital city of Japan, but there was something special about this mission. Instead of being at 20 or 30 thousand feet, they would be at a very low altitude and very vulnerable to antiaircraft fire.

Russell Vifquain had already done more than his duty. In December 1941, almost three and one-half years earlier, he had been on his way to the Philippines with a flight of B-17 bombers. The surprise attack on Pearl Harbor had changed everything. He was sent to navigate a new B-26 Martin Maruader bomber operating out of Alaska. The B-26 was a twin-engine, cigar-shaped plane, which in the early days was affectionately known as the "Flying Coffin," and this was its maiden voyage into combat.[1]

Vifquain flew 30 bombing missions through the bleak and frigid Alaskan weather, repulsing the Japanese landings at Dutch Harbor as well as Attu and Kiska. With that campaign having been successfully completed, he was on his second tour of combat duty in the Pacific.

This raid over Tokyo was calculated to do great damage to the city, and it did. The low-altitude bombing raid by the 343 Super Fortresses dropping incendiary bombs completely burned out 16 square miles of Tokyo, including 18 percent of the city's industrial area. The Japanese people were completely unable to cope with the new tactic of firebombing over a wide area. The hundreds of air raid drills they had conducted since that first air raid by Jimmie Doolittle came to nought. Japanese fire-fighting equipment was primitive, and the efforts of the firemen were useless against the holocaust which befell the city. Dwellings made of paper and packing-case wood flared and vanished like matches. Water in the canals began to boil. Clouds of steam rose into the air to mingle with thick drifts of smoke and soot above the city. Charred bodies of men, women, and children were strewn all over the city in the raging inferno. In the end, 83,000 people died and another 41,000 were injured. Some 267,000 buildings lay in smoldering ashes as a result of the most destructive raid in history.

Admiral Yamamoto had said that "if there were large scale air raids, there is no telling what would happen." Now they knew but, even with such devastation from a single raid, the Japanese people showed no intention to surrender. Just four days later, Juny was on another raid—this time, over Nagoya. Then he was on more raids over Tokyo.

On the night of 13 May 1945, there was a great deal of hurried activity around the tiny island of Saipan as XXI Bomber Command prepared for another raid over Japan. It was Juny's 17th mission in B-29s and he was lead navigator for the 524 planes of the command. The big silver ships moved into take-off position one after another shortly after midnight for an early morning strike on the city of Nagoya. Everything went in routine fashion as aircraft roared down the runway and headed out over the water in the black night.

The crew settled into their various responsibilities for the five and one-half hour flight to the target area. By now, these missions had become routine. But as they started their climb to flight altitude, the number one engine began to backfire. However, the powerful plane easily made the climb and led the formation at 16,000 feet until the number four engine started to backfire. They had just crossed the coastline of Japan when the pilot feathered the propeller and left the formation. With so much engine trouble, it was obvious that they could not proceed with the formation. Dawn was just breaking as they headed back to Saipan. At that point, the commander of the plane had the bomb load salvoed. Some of the falling bombs struck the rear bomb-bay door, damaging it so that it would not close properly.

They had flown south for about an hour when the number three engine also started to backfire and the plane started losing altitude at the rate of 400 feet per minute. At that juncture, all of the loose gear and equipment was stacked near the bulkhead so that it could be thrown overboard in case it became necessary to ditch the plane. It had become apparent to everyone that they were confronted with a serious problem. Soon Juny was able to establish their position as being about one hour's flying time from the tiny island of Iwo Jima. The island, which was a mere four and one-half miles long, lay midway between Saipan and Japan. It had been wrested from the Japanese only two months before at the frightful cost of the lives of 5,000 US Marines.

Before Iwo Jima had been secured by the Marines, Japanese radar stations on the island had been able to warn the homeland of approaching B-29s. Americans had eliminated the Japanese radar outposts, and Iwo Jima provided a base for US fighters to escort our bombers to Japan. It also provided a haven for some 2,251 crippled Super Fortresses on the return trip from raids on Japan.

It was nearly noon on 14 May 1945, when Major Vifquain's plane approached the island. The plane's commander had instructed the radio operator to send a message giving their expected time of arrival. The clouds were so low that visibility was almost nil, and the commander knew that if they went below the clouds he would be forced to land immediately. There was no way that he could regain altitude, given the condition of the engines. If they went below the clouds and were not in line with the runway, a crash would be inevitable. Therefore, the commander decided to make two passes across the island allowing half of the crew to bail out on each pass. This plan became impossible, however, when the number one engine caught fire. With the aid of Vifquain, the pilot directed the plane over the island and gave the order to bail out.

The crew members bailed out in clouds so thick that they were unable to see one another after leaving the plane. Those in the rear of the plane dived out the rear door while those in the forward part, including Vifquain, left through the nosewheel well. The airmen were unable to tell whether they were descending over land or water. The commander, who was the last to leave the burning plane, bailed out just 10 seconds before it exploded. He was seven miles away from the island, but was soon picked up by a rescue boat.

Four others were also rescued from the water while five had landed safely on the island. Yet, there was no trace of Maj Russell Vifquain or Sgt Donald A. Barnes, the tail gunner. Vifquain was seen bailing out through the nosewheel well, but nobody saw him after that. He had vanished.[2]

Notes

1. The first B-26 flew in November 1940 and was considered one of the most modern aircraft of the time. Equipped with two large Pratt and Whitney engines that produced a total of 1,850 horsepower, the early production models of the B-26 coupled speed and power with a short 65-foot wingspan that made it a challenge to fly. Christened the Marauder by its builder, the Martin Aviation Company, it was known as the Murderer by apprehensive crews. The first B-26 transition school was established at MacDill field in Tampa, Florida. Referring to the number of planes that novice B-26 pilots spun into the nearby waters of the Gulf, "one a day in Tampa Bay" became an expression well known throughout the AAF. A 6-foot wing extension markedly improved the B-26's handling characteristics. As a specialized ground attack aircraft redesignated the A-26, this improved aircraft saw useful service as late as the Vietnam War. The early checkered career of the B-26 is recounted in Geoffrey Perret, *Winged Victory: The Army Air Forces in World War II* (New York: Random House, 1993), 94–96.

2. Missing Air Crew Report 35-19 9577, National Archives, Suitland Reference Branch, Maryland, 4 November 1944.

INDIVIDUAL COMBAT RECORD

VIRGUAIN, RUSSELL M

NAME	RANK	ASN	CREW POSITION & NO.
	1st Lt	O-809919	
73rd WING	499th GROUP	Sq SQDN	103L SSN

DATE DEPT. USA 25 Nov 1944 AUTH: DATE ARRV. THIS THEATRE

CREDITS

DATE	MISSION NUMBER	TARGET	AIRPLANE NUMBER	RESULT	SORTIES INDIV	SORTIES TOTAL	COMBAT HRS INDIV	COMBAT HRS TOTAL	INITIALS	E/A CLAIMS KILL	PROB	DAM	REMARKS
NOV 24 44	7	TOKYO	V24 (42224)	A		1	14:30	14:30					#2 & 3 ENG FAILURE
DEC 3 44	10	TOKYO	V-1 (47265)	P (FROM ISE AC T)	0	1	9:00	23:30					FUEL TRANS SYSTEM FAIL
DEC 27 44	13A	NAGOYA	V51 (245)	T	0	1	7:45	31:15					(CREDIT TOWARDS AWARD) ONLY
DEC 22 44	14	NAGOYA	V51 (245)	P	1	2	13:45	45:00					
FEB 27 44	16	TOKYO	V23 (4844)	P (MARSH ZERO-PRO) T	1	3	14:00	59:00					
FEB 23 45	WSM		V22 (464)	P	1	4	14:05	73:05					#3 ENG OUT
MAR 9 45	29	TOKYO	V29 (3465)	P	1	5	14:35	87:40					
MAR 13 45	31	OSAKI	V41 (465)	P	1	6	14:05	101:45					
MAR 19 45	33	NAGOYA	V15 (5340)	P	1	7	13:05	114:50					
MAR 24 45	34	NAGOYA	V28 (3465)	A (KRU SHU T)	0	8	1:15	116:05					ENG TROUBLE - 3 BOMBS NOT ON
MAR 27 45	35		V48 (4150)	T	1	8	15:15	131:20					TANK SAFETY SWITCHES
APR 13 45	42	TOKYO	V54 (9580)	P	1	9	13:10	144:30					
APR 7 45	44	IZUMI AF	V26 (4775)	P	1	10	14:35	159:05					
APR 4 45	WSM	IITA AF	VL8	P		11	11:45	172:50					
APR 17 45	55	IZUMI	V-67 (4120)	P		12	14:15	187:15					
APR 29 45	ESCORT	TOKY	V-36 (4663)	C	0	12	6:35	193:40					
MAY 14 45	174-69	NAGOYA	V-27 (9260)	A	?		11:45	205:25					ABANDONED SHIP OVER IWO. MISSING

-OVER-

KEY TO RESULT COLUMN: P-PRIMARY   S-SECONDARY   T-TARGET OF OPPORTUNITY   A-ABORT   C-COMPLETE NO TARGET   L-LAST RESORT

Figure 3.   Individual Combat Record

Boselli and the *Sacred Cow*

> Hey diddle diddle
> The cat and the fiddle
> The cow jumped over the moon.

The cow was sacred, alright. It did not really jump over the moon, but it came closer to it than any other cow. In fact, it was not really a cow—it was an airplane. It was the personal aircraft of possibly the most important person in the world at the time.

No president of the United States had sported an official airplane before Franklin Delano Roosevelt. And in 1943, there was considerable debate as to whether the chief executive of the United States should fly. However, Roosevelt had a flair for the dramatic. He was the first US president to visit the continent of Africa and the first president since Abraham Lincoln to visit a battle theater in time of war. None before him had ever left the US in time of war.

The first airplane flight of a US president took place on 11 January 1943. The plane was a Pan American flying boat, the flight was from the Dinner Key Seaplane Base in Miami to the Casablanca Conference in northern Africa. By coincidence, Charlie Lunn was teaching air cadets the techniques of celestial navigation at that Pan American Airways base. Later that year, classified documents known as Project 51 were sent from Washington, D.C., to the Douglas Aircraft Company in Santa Monica, California. Approximately nine months later, on 12 June 1944, the "Cow" was born. On that date, the first presidential aircraft was flown from the Douglas Plant in Santa Monica to National Airport, Washington, D.C. It was a four-engine, propeller driven, C-54 airplane. No one ever expected that the official aircraft of the president of the United States would be called the *Sacred Cow*. It might have been christened The Flying White House except for irreverent Washington newspaper correspondents. Official attempts to discourage use of the name *Sacred Cow* as "undignified" were to little avail.

The name was never painted on the airplane, nor was the name ever officially accepted. From the beginning to the end, however, it was known as the *Sacred Cow*.

There were problems in designing the president's plane because President Franklin D. Roosevelt, who had been stricken with polio at age 31, could walk only with crutches. He could not climb the steps of the plane. Designers considered that it would be totally inappropriate to carry the most important man in the world on and off his plane like a baby. If designers used long ramps for his wheelchair, it would foretell his arrival wherever he traveled. For these reasons, Project 51 provided for a battery-operated elevator, located aft of the main passenger cabin, which could lift a passenger directly from the ground to the cabin-floor level of the aircraft.

More than that, the interior of the plane was laid out so that Roosevelt could move easily to all parts of the cabin in his wheelchair. A removable set of inclined rails allowed him to be rolled up to the cockpit between the pilot and copilot.

The president's private stateroom measured 7½ x 12 feet. Among the special furnishings was an upholstered swivel chair which was within easy reach of an oxygen mask, reading lights, and a telephone to the pilot's compartment. At that time, air-to-ground telephone service was not in use; nor was the plane pressurized. A conference table was in the middle of his stateroom, while on one side were four maps on rollers. There were also enlarged flying instruments, including an air speed indicator, an altimeter, a compass, and a clock. There was no air conditioning, so an electric fan perched atop a cabinet.

A large bulletproof window was an additional feature of this section of the plane. Ironically, although this window would afford protection against an assassin's bullet, the surrounding skin of the aircraft would hardly have stopped an ice pick.

The Crew

Nothing but the finest and most competent flyers would be suitable for the crew of the president's aircraft. Through the selection process, Maj Henry ("Hank") T. Myers, a military-trained pilot who had years of experience with American

Airlines, was designated as the president's chief pilot. Elmer Smith was the copilot and Charlie Lunn's star student from the Class of 40-A, Theodore J. Boselli, was the navigator for the *Sacred Cow*.

Boselli was not like any of his other classmates. He had been born of Irish and Italian parents in the Bowery district of downtown Manhattan. Physically, the Italian showed through much more than the Irish. He had the dark eyes and curly dark hair typical of many Italians—but his nature was that of a happy Irishman. Never ruffled or worried, he had breezed through the academic part of navigational school with ease and aplomb. To him, the complicated course was like child's play. On an examination that took the remainder of the class two days to complete, Boselli rolled up his charts toward the end of the first day, deposited them on Charlie's desk, and strolled out as if he had decided not to finish the test. Nevertheless, when the grades were posted, his grade fell in the range of 98 to 100 percent.

In the early days of the Great Depression, his mother had been his sole support. He was later able to get a job working as a delivery boy, but his mother wanted more than that for her son. She was able to get him enrolled in Clemson University in South Carolina. There, by his own admission, he was more of an athlete than a student. He got an athletic scholarship, which made it possible for him to complete college and get a degree in engineering. He was on the baseball team and was regional bantamweight boxing champion. Even though he was a graduate of Clemson University, an unmistakable Bowery accent stayed with him throughout his military career.

Boselli's reputation as an outstanding navigator soon became recognized, and he was assigned to fly special missions for dignitaries from National Airport in Washington, D.C.

His first big mission was to navigate Ambassador Averill Harriman to Moscow in the fall of 1941, before the US was involved in World War II. Officials determined that the safest route from London to Moscow would be to travel north past Norway, east, and then south over Archangel to Moscow. The 3,000-mile trip would take them well above the Arctic Circle, where no plane had ever flown before. It would be a real challenge for Boselli's talents. In addition to the navigational problems, there was the matter of communications. The US military was certain that the Soviets were not familiar with the twin-tailed B-24 bomber, so it became very important to apprise them of the arrival over the USSR of friendly American planes. The Soviet ambassador accompanied the Harriman plane to assist with communications.

Boselli's masterful navigation directed the flight northward up the North Sea, across the Norwegian Sea, around Sweden and Finland, to Archangel. At that point, they were 600 miles north of Moscow. Everything had worked out as planned, but when the crew tried to make radio contact with Moscow, there was no response. In spite of their plans and preparations, something had gone wrong. To proceed to the Moscow airport without communicating with someone would be courting disaster.

To quickly solve their problem of warning the Moscow Airport of their impending arrival, they resorted to an ingenious but simple process. The Soviet ambassador wrote out a message in Russian, "American airplane landing at Moscow," put it in a tin can and tied a long cloth streamer on it. The plane then flew low over an airport to the north of Moscow, dropped the message and flew straight to Moscow where they landed without incident. There they were feted with a state dinner honoring Harriman and were introduced to Joseph Stalin, then our ally and supposed friend.

When it was time to depart, the Soviets directed the Americans on a southern route to Baghdad, providing them with a strip map covering five to 10 miles in width. They apparently did not desire to share Soviet geographical information with her allies. The expedition flew south to the Black Sea, Baghdad, and Cairo, and then back to Washington, D.C.

Rescue from Philippines and Java

On 7 December 1941, at the outbreak of World War II, Boselli was headed from Washington, D.C., to Cairo, Egypt. The diplomat on board was Ambassador William Bullitt, who was to take a tour of Jerusalem and Beirut, Lebanon. In Beirut, the crew received an urgent message to leave the Ambassador in Cairo and depart for the East Indies. They proceeded to Calcutta and to Rangoon, Burma, where Gen Claire Chennault's "Flying Tigers" were flying aerial missions in their P-40s against the Japanese.

By the year's end, Boselli's plane had arrived in Australia with a load of much-needed .50-caliber machine-gun ammunition. The B-17s of the 19th Bombardment Group had been driven out of Clark Field and were flying missions out of Mindanao (in the Philippines), Java, and Australia. However, Japanese forces had continued moving south until it was necessary to evacuate the Philippines. The few B-17s that survived were being flown night and day by the battle-weary crews. Gen Lewis Brereton directed Boselli's crew to evacuate crew members from the Philippines.

For the next couple of months, Bosellis plane flew night missions evacuating aircrew members and technicians out of the Philippines to Australia. His last flight brought out crew members of the PT boats that had evacuated General MacArthur from Corregidor to Mindanao. When they completed that assignment, Boselli and crew were next assigned to evacuate personnel from Java to Australia.

Junketeering

Junketeering by US senators and congressmen may have started in 1943. The practice got off to a rollicking start with the Truman Committee going on a three-month junket around the world. Sen Harry S Truman, later to become president of the United States, had given distinguished service to his country by cutting waste in the national defense program. With America deeply committed in World War II, it became important for the US Senate to learn more about world affairs. The blue ribbon committee, comprised of Senators Henry Cabot Lodge, A. B. ("Happy") Chandler, Richard Russel, Ralph O. Brewster, and James M. Mead, was dispatched by Harry Truman. He did not make the trip, even though the committee bore his name: Truman Committee. Though this account of the junket was never entered into the Congressional Record, navigator Boselli's observations of the committee's activities are as follows:

Each one thought he was king. So when one guy did something to us, like hold us up on takeoff or make a delay. Then the other guy got mad. I'll tell you in plain English that this affected us. We were the crew, you know. They would screw up our take-off time and everything else. There were times when we could only land during daylight hours, and we had this planned out. If we didn't take off this time, we weren't going to get there; so we couldn't go there. These airports weren't like they are nowadays with GCA landings and lights. But they just didn't understand. So one guy would stall and the other guy would get mad, and the next day we'd be later, so then everybody was late. So we cancelled the flight. We did this to them a couple of times until finally they got smart and decided they had better show up when we said what the latest time we could take off was.

Henry Cabot Lodge was a nice-looking gentleman. He was a gentleman, sort of aloof, but a gentleman. He did not say much to us one way or the other and never gave us any problems. There's one thing I do remember about him; after three months, he wrote us a letter and thanked us for the trip. He was the only one. Yes, he was aloof, the type you couldn't get close to. But what the hell, we weren't supposed to get close. We were crew members, flyers.

Happy Chandler was a real nice, friendly guy. He liked us because we had flown him before. He couldn't stand to fly and was scared to death. He admitted it. But he hung in there.[1]

After navigating the Truman Committee to England, Italy, Africa, India, and China, Boselli was back to flying special missions worldwide. Then came a call for him to lead a squadron of A-24 medium bombers across the South Atlantic from West Palm Beach to Africa and then to Cairo. Three of the 12 were lost at sea between West Palm Beach and Puerto Rico. Others were lost in the African desert, due to heavy dust fouling the engines. The trip was an utter fiasco, typical of the daring and desperate aerial actions in the early part of World War II.

When Boselli returned to the US, General Arnold, chief of the US Air Corps, ordered him to England to make a study of navigational problems in the Eighth Air Force. Boselli navigated on a few bombing missions and gave his analysis of the situation. By his own admission, he "didn't have a very good reception from the boys who were having the problems there."

Finally, the thing that Boselli had dreamed of for years materialized. He had visions of navigating for the president of the United States. At the time he learned of Project 51, he was flying combat missions in the Eighth Air Force in England. Since he was overseas at the time, he was afraid that someone else would get the assignment.

After days of agony, the nagging worry was put to rest when a message from Washington told him, "Rush back home." He said, "Boy, did I rush back and I got on the crew."

One of his first important missions as navigator of the *Sacred Cow* was to take Gen George C. Marshall, the chief of staff of the United States Army, from Washington, D.C., to his triumphant reentry into Paris. During the previous months, Boselli had been navigating missions worldwide. By that time, his reputation as a crack navigator was secure and General Marshall knew that the president's crew was the best in the military services. Even under the best of conditions, however, things did not always work out as planned. Meteorology and navigational aids were relatively primitive at the time.

Marshall's plane flew the Atlantic from Washington. Boselli was able to visibly establish his exact position as he crossed Ireland. Forecast winds had been fairly accurate. Based on them, he estimated the time he would arrive in Paris. It was scheduled to be an early morning arrival, but the estimated time of arrival (ETA) caused everyone to move up his schedule for an earlier arrival time.

The return of America's top military officer, for the first time since the Allies had liberated the French capital, was a big event. The star-studded reception committee included Gen Charles de Gaulle, Gen Omar Bradley, and a host of international dignitaries waiting in the early morning cold.

It did not take Boselli long to learn that a sudden change in the direction and velocity of the wind had cut down his speed dramatically. A low pressure area had moved in a different direction than had been forecast. Instead of a 35 mile an hour tailwind, the plane had a 70 mile an hour head wind. That made a great difference in their speed.

Boselli was, at first, embarrassed, then sick. There was not anything he or anybody else could do about it. It was too late.

It was one of the most important flights he ever made and by far the worst in his military career as a navigator.

As Boselli said, "When you are transporting dignitaries, they don't care how long it takes you to get to a place. The important thing with VIPs is that when you say you are going to be there, be there." In this case, Gen George Catlett Marshall kept his reception committee waiting for one and one-half hours.

A later trip was much less embarrassing when Boselli navigated Gen Dwight D. Eisenhower on his triumphant return to the United States in June of 1945 after the Allied victory in Europe.

The president of the United States did not like to travel by air. Franklin Delano Roosevelt had been assistant secretary of the Navy and he preferred surface craft to flying. He frequently traveled by battleship and had his personal aircraft, the *Sacred Cow*, haul the dignitaries to his various official functions.

The fact is that with all of the elaborate preparation, electric elevator, bulletproof window, and rails for pulling up into the cockpit between the pilot and the copilot, President Franklin Roosevelt rode in the *Sacred Cow* just one time. For the historic Yalta Conference, he had traveled to Malta on a battleship. From Malta, he made his first and only flight in the *Sacred Cow*. The flight was from Malta to Yalta on 3 February 1945. The flight was made only after practice runs with heavy fighter escort between Malta and Yalta. The president boarded his plane late at night and arrived at Yalta early in the morning. Stalin and Churchill were there to meet the president for that historic conference.

On another trip when Roosevelt went to Hawaii to meet with General MacArthur, he traveled by battleship and the *Cow*, as it was affectionately referred to by the crew, tagged along carrying Secret Service agents.

Boselli observed that the president was in exceedingly ill health and considered that as one of the reasons he did not like to fly. The president died on 12 April, just a couple of months after the Yalta Conference.

With the death of President Roosevelt, presidential flying took on a new color. Harry Truman loved to fly, and he made his first flight on the *Sacred Cow* on 5 May 1945. One year later he did something that no other president had ever done.

146

Buzz the White House

On a hot summer afternoon, President Truman, his wife Bess, and daughter Margaret were sitting on the roof of the White House watching an air show. P-80 aircraft of the Army Air Corps were putting on a spectacular acrobatic air show south of the city. The president left the party because he was to fly to Independence, Missouri, that afternoon to visit his aged mother. His limousine quickly delivered him to his waiting plane at Bolling Field just across the Potomac River from National Airport. The acrobatic planes were grounded during the presidents take off, but the president had been inspired by their antics.

As his plane was gaining altitude, the president moved to his favorite posititon where he could visit with the crew. But he was there for another reason. "You know, Hank," he addressed the pilot Henry ("Hank") Meyers, "Bess and Margaret are over there on the roof of the White House. Could we just dive down there?" The crew was aghast at such a request and waited for the captains reply.

"You know, Mr. President, if I did that I would never fly again." Myers knew that the White House was a restricted zone and there would be a stiff penalty with the possibility of being grounded forever for such a refraction of flight regulations.

"Would it make any difference if I told you to do it?" insisted the president.

Myers knew that as captain of the plane, he had the power to overrule any passenger, even the president of the United States.

"What do you say? It is something I have always wanted to do."

"Well, somebody is going to catch hell and I'm going to blame you," answered the pilot in mock seriousness.

With that Myers wheeled the big four-engine transport around from about 3,000 feet above the Potomac River and headed directly toward the White House with a roar that could be heard for miles. Down, down, down it went through 2,000 feet, 1,000 feet, and leveled off to roar over the White House with throttles to the wall at 500 feet.

The president, with his face pressed against the window, was grinning from ear to ear as he saw the White House observers petrified with fear at the sight of the big bird descending upon them. But as the plane flew past, they could easily recognize it as the *Sacred Cow*. During wartime, it bore no presidential seal and no special markings.

The first foray was so satisfying that they had to do it again. Again from 3,000 feet the *Sacred Cow* bore in on the residence of the chief executive of the United States. This time Bess and Margaret, having recognized the plane, knew that it was Harry Truman having some excitement. They waved and shouted in glee as the plane made its second pass before it headed away into the western sky.

Boselli gave Myers the heading for the trip to Missouri as the passengers settled back for the long trip. If things were peaceful on the airplane, it was not so back in the nations capitol as phones at the Civil Aeronautics Administration, the Secret Service, the city police stations, and the Army Air Force were ringing off the hook. All concerns were put to rest when the operations office at Bolling Field announced that the intruding plane was the presidents and that the president was aboard.[2]

About Mr Truman, Boselli said,

Mr. Truman—a tremendous individual! I like him, personally. I don't agree with his politics, but he's nice. Politics—he's a different type. He's not a politician. Maybe he used to be a politician; I don't know. But anyhow, he was a real nice guy. We flew him quite a bit locally, into Kansas City and back, down to Key West and back. We did a lot of that. . . . They were real nice folks, what I call plain old folks. . . . We had to fly around the States quite a bit, and a lot of things. . . . The only mission while I was there was the Potsdam Conference, I think it was the only big official deal overseas. We brought him into Berlin and spent a little time there and then came back. And we did a lot of stateside flying, but I got to know his whole family real well.

The wife and daughter were nothing spectacular, just plain old good family. It had nothing to do with whether they were a president or a president's wife, it was just a nice old family relation. I don't know how else to say it. They were real nice to us. We like them. And they treated us just like we were part of the family. We were part of the family, too, I suppose. We did fly his mother. It was the only time she ever flew on an airplane. She was somewhere between ninety and ninety-two years of age, as I recall. We picked her up at Kansas City and brought her back to Washington. She was a tremendous lady. We lucked out, of course. The weather was good. But she really enjoyed it.[3]

That was on Mother's Day in 1945. The electric elevator was used that day for her convenience.

Upon retirement of the *Sacred Cow* on 4 December 1961, the ceremony at Andrews Air Force Base, Maryland, resembled the pomp and military customs of the retirement of a general from active duty. None ever had a more colorful career.

- It was the first official presidential plane.

- It had borne the flags of 51 counties it had visited.

- It claimed the first nonstop flight from the United Kingdom to Washington, D.C.

- Among its passengers had been Presidents Roosevelt, Truman, Hoover, and Eisenhower, as well as Madame Chiang Kai-shek, Winston Churchill, Dr Edward Beneš of Czechoslovakia, and General Skorshi of Poland. Theodore J. Boselli had been her navigator.

On 1 July 1945, Boselli navigated a new presidential aircraft from the Santa Monica Douglas Aircraft Plant to the National Airport in Washington, D.C. To avoid its being christened the *Sacred Cow* II, the *Independence* was selected as the official name for President Truman's personal aircraft. It was very appropriate because that was the name of his old hometown back in Missouri.

By that time, Boselli had been navigating dignitaries all over the world for more than six years. He decided to leave the assignment as navigator for the president and go back to regular Air Force duties. Later he made a short tour of combat duty in B-29 bombers over Korea. At the time of his retirement from the Air Force with the rank of colonel, he was serving as logistics officer for the 15th Air Force.

It had been a long road for the kid from the lower east side of Manhattan, a champion boxer at Clemson University and a champion navigator in Charlie Lunn's class. As an angel of mercy, he had flown missions rescuing aircrew members from the Philippines and Java. He had flown combat missions in the Eighth Air Force over Europe and B-29 missions over Korea— and he had probably navigated for more world dignitaries than any person in history.

In retirement, he made his home at Tustin, California.

Notes

1. Theodore J. Boselli, interview with Harris N. Done, California State College, Fullerton, Oral History Program, Community History Project, 27 April 1971, 89.
2. Theodore J. Boselli, interview with author, Tustin, Calif., 1972.
3. Boselli interview with Done, 13.

New Hope

After a weary night of numbness, a quiet dawn came over Corregidor. Across the waters, I (Ed Whitcomb) could see the outline of Mt. Mariveles against the distant sky with its ever-present ring of clouds hanging above its peak. The weary bodies of the men began to move as first one and then another became conscious that a new day was upon us.

A Japanese soldier broke the silence of the morning with a command, "Standing!"

We struggled to our feet and followed instructions to march to the airstrip where we had been the day before. There the Japanese furnished a variety of yard and garden implements—shovels, hoes, rakes, and picks. Our assignment was to fill in the bomb craters on the airstrip to make it useable for Japanese planes.

We toiled in the boiling hot sun until noon as we filled in the bomb craters and smoothed off the airfield. Then came good news. We were going to eat. I had no idea of the last time I had eaten. It had surely been a long time ago. The Japanese guard handed each of us a can of American Army C rations. I wondered where they had been kept all of that time because I could not remember having seen such rations before.

During our break for food, someone said something to the guard about international law. The arrogant little guard blurted out, "Japanese law is international law!" He then continued to express his unfavorable opinion of Americans in very explicit terms.

The Japanese soldiers were jubilant at their victory over us. It somehow seemed that they had not expected it to happen. It had happened and they were in control. There was no question about that. They were all smaller in size than their American prisoners, but they were tough jungle warriors. They had fought a long and hard battle in the jungles of Bataan. Many had perished there from gunfire, malaria fever, and other tropical diseases. They had also suffered great losses when

151

they invaded Corregidor. That was all in the past. Now they were enjoying power and authority beyond anything they could have ever imagined.

We continued our work until late in the evening. Then again we were given the order to sleep. This time several hundred of us laid on the level ground of the runway and had no trouble in finding rest. The following day we continued leveling the airfield runway. Toward evening we observed a small Japanese plane winging in over Manila Bay to make a perfect landing on the newly resurrected Kindley Field. Corregidor belonged to the Japanese.

With our work completed, we marched in a column of fours back toward Malinta Tunnel. There we entered a crescent-shaped area on the south shore of the island where we joined thousands of other American and Filipino prisoners. It was the 92d garage area and it was to be our home as long as we remained on the island of Corregidor. Midst the teeming crowd I found John Renka and Jim Dey, my friends who had escaped from Bataan with me a month before. I had not seen them since our arrival on the island. At that time we had been elated because we thought we were going to Australia by submarine to get back to our outfit. At this meeting we were sad and dejected because we knew there was no longer any hope for getting back into the war. For us the war had ended.

The total number of people in the 92d garage area was 11,000 soldiers, sailors, and marines. We were confined into an area about the size of one city block with hardly room to move about. At night when we laid down on the ground to sleep, it was impossible to keep paths open to move from one part of the area to another without stepping on outstretched arms or legs.

We took up quarters with some Marine officers outside the northwest corner of one of the two large metal buildings. They had been small seaplane hangers in days gone by. Being on the south side of the island along the coast, the hangars had been protected from the artillery fire from Bataan. A clinic was set up just inside the building where the sick and dying were laid out on the cement floor. The outside wall of the building had been torn away so the people in the sick bay were plainly visible.

The hills around the camp gave the area the atmosphere of an oven as the May sun blazed down on the unprotected bodies of the prisoners. There were no tents and no protection whatsoever from the elements except for the small percentage of prisoners in the hangars. Some few of us found relief from the heat by going into the water at the edge of the camp. There, armed guards along the shore watched our every move.

For relief from the sweltering heat of the prison camp area, it was possible to volunteer for work details outside the area. We would ordinarily go in groups of 50 or 60 men. Much of the labor entailed carrying stores of American food to Japanese ships. The stores included rice, cornmeal, and a large variety of canned goods. It was possible to poke a hole in a bag and fill our pockets with rice or cornmeal. We could also try to pry a board off a crate, get a can of food, and hide it inside our shirts. We knew that the penalty for getting caught was very severe. We had seen other prisoners being punished in a variety of ways for such misconduct. Some were required to stand in the sun holding a rock high above their heads for hours at a time. Stealing was a chance we had to take for survival, however. During the time I was in the 92d garage area, I never knew of any food being provided by the Japanese for our area of the camp. We would pool our resources with the marines. Then we would cook the food over an open fire in rusty cans, or whatever else we could find.

Nobody escaped dysentery or "Guam blisters," which gathered in clusters under our arms and on our legs. With the heat and the ever-present flies, we surely existed in a dazed condition of weakness and lethargy.

There were rumors of prisoner exchange and of escape—rumors that are always present among men when there is nothing more to hope for. I made the acquaintance of a young marine by the name of William Harris, who was from Versailles, Kentucky. Bill was a graduate of the US Naval Academy, Class of 1939, and he had been commander of a rifle company during the Japanese invasion of Corregidor. Tall and thin, he gave the appearance of being a very resourceful person. I was impressed with him for the reason that he was dead serious about escaping from Corregidor.

Our problem was that we were on an island with water all around us. We could see the shore of Cavite eight miles to the south of us, and we knew that it was about two and one-half miles back to Bataan on the north of the island. Swimming the eight miles to Cavite was out of the question for us, but we considered that it would be possible to swim to Bataan. We would first have to find a way to get out of camp and to the north shore of Corregidor.

I talked with Harris at length about how we might be able to get away. We discussed it and pondered the problems, over and over. Other people I talked to included John Renka, Jim Dey, and a marine by the name of Jack Hawkins. At night, Bill would insist to me that we attempt to slip out of camp past the guards and up over the hill to the north shore. We both knew of the machine-gun nests and guard posts as well as the barbed wire fence strewn about our area. "We can make it," he would insist. "Let's go tonight."

We were desperate. We wanted to go, but I felt that the odds were too great against us on any effort to slip past the sentries at night. We would surely be shot. On the other hand, there was a question about how long we could survive in the prison camp. More and more wretched bodies were being brought to the makeshift aid station next to us. The death rate in camp was on the increase.

Bill and I walked to the water's edge and looked far across the south channel to the Cavite shore. Then we waded out into the water to swim back and forth within the limits the watchful guards had prescribed. We did it for several days with the hope of developing our swimming strength.

In the evening back in our camp area, I happened to be gazing into the sick bay area near our location when I noticed that one of the patients had stopped breathing. It all happened so quietly and peaceably that nobody else seemed to notice it. He was lying on his back on the cement floor surrounded by about 11,000 prisoners, and he had left them. His body and soul had found peace, and I thought for a moment that he was one of the lucky ones. His cares had come to an end. There would be no more starvation for him, no more fretting under the steaming hot Corregidor sun. Soon his body was taken away as dozens of others had been taken away. For him the war had ended. For us it seemed that we must make a move while we still had the strength to do it—or die!

May 22d was a happy and exciting day for me because that was the day we were going to try to make our getaway. At about 2:00 P.M. 60 officers and men filed out of the barbed wire barricade past the machine-gun nests to go out on a wood-gathering detail. We were accompanied by an armed Japanese guard. At a point about 200 yards from camp, Bill dropped down into a deep foxhole when no one was looking. He called for me and seeing that the guard was not looking our way, I joined him in the underground hideaway. Apparently, nobody noticed our disappearance from the group. We waited almost breathlessly while our comrades swept across the hillside gathering sticks.

We waited. Would the Japanese soldiers come looking for us? Would they miss us back in camp? Many worries crossed our minds as we hid, waiting for darkness. The afternoon was an eternity. The sun seemed to hang in the sky as if it would never go down. Then, when darkness came, it seemed as if everything had happened quickly. The sun was gone. Darkness came and it was time for us to make our move.

We stealthily made our way down the hill to the north shore, watching and listening for the calamity which would bring an end to our trip. Where was that sentry or machine-gun nest? Our eyes and ears strained, waiting to hear a Japanese screaming at us—or a shot which would bring it all to an end. It was as if the world was ours. All was quiet except for the sound of the waves lapping against the shore. We crept down to the shore, lowered ourselves into the water, and started the long two and one-half mile swim back to Bataan and to our freedom.

Swimming was good. Our progress was good. A light far across the water on Bataan would guide us to our destination. We made our way toward that light with a feeling that we were making good progress. We had swum for about two hours when the waves began to get choppier and larger. The atmosphere thickened until we were no longer able to see our guiding light. After a while longer, it started to sprinkle. Then it started to rain. The waves became so high and so violent that I was unable to communicate with Bill. I screamed and

155

screamed in the darkness of the storm, with a feeling that our long battle for survival had been lost.

Then, at long last, the rain ceased—almost as suddenly as it had started. I could hear Bill's voice in the distance. We swam until we were closer together and then vowed that we would not get far enough apart to get lost from each other again. But we had no sense of direction. We could not see our light. There was nothing to do but tread water until we could find out which way to go.

After awhile, we were again able to see a light—and the best part about it was that it seemed to be much closer. We swam with a new enthusiasm until suddenly we both became aware of the outline of a large ship. The light was on the ship and the ship was tied up in the North Mine Dock of Corregidor.

We estimated that we had been in the water more than two hours, and we were no more than one-fourth of a mile from where we had started. The demoralizing thing was the knowledge that we were not more than a couple hundred yards from shore. The strong tide had carried us westward toward the China Sea. We had a choice. We could swim back to shore and rest before taking a fresh start, or we could go on. The choice was easy for us. We again turned to the north and started swimming with a new determination. Swimming became mechanical. On and on and on, like walking, hour after hour. We did not swim hard or fast but we kept a steady gait.

At long last, we sighted a barge in the water off to the right of our course. It seemed to be anchored, and we considered swimming to it with the hope that we could rest for awhile. However, as we drew near, we realized that we were much closer to the Bataan shore than we had thought. It was then growing light, and we were able to clearly see bushes and trees on the shoreline. It gave us new energy, and we struggled on until we were able to crawl out of the water and onto the shores of Bataan. We dragged ourselves into a clump of bushes and collapsed, wet and exhausted—and happy that our battle against the sea was over.

When we awoke, the sun was low in the western sky. We had slept all day. We looked back across the waters of the channel to Corregidor and rejoiced that we had freed ourselves from that terrible prison camp. We were free and it was a great feeling.

This should be the happy end of a story, but it is only the beginning of difficulties beyond anything we could have foreseen. We learned what a lot of other escapees learned: Getting out of prison camp was the easiest part of all. That is where the real battle begins. From there, we had to cope with the jungle, starvation, malaria fever, hostile and treacherous natives, and, of course, the Japanese. We had our battles and victories and defeats with all of them.

Bataan to Santo Tomas

Our ultimate destination was China. The plan was to walk north across the middle of the Bataan Peninsula. Thus we (Harris and Whitcomb) would avoid Japanese soldiers who occupied the coastal areas. The main obstacle in our proposed route was 4,000 foot Mt. Mariveles, which we knew would be difficult to cross.

The night grew dark as we made our way along the trail to the village of Cabcaben. There we found some friendly Filipinos and persuaded them to provide us with a meal of rice and fish. They were nervous and urged us to leave quickly because a Japanese patrol would be coming through the village soon. We carried the food with us and quickly slipped into the dark jungle.

The unfamiliar area increased our anxiety as we pushed our way into the dark night. After a couple of hours we became so ensnared in the tropical jungle that we were unable to move very far in any direction. We had no choice but to lie down on the ground and sleep until daylight. It was of no concern to us that adventurer Frank Buck was said to have captured his largest python snake there in the jungles of Bataan.

At dawn we were able to continue the climb up the mountain. Toward evening we became concerned because we had walked all day without finding anything to eat. We had expected to find tropical fruit, but there was none. Hunger and exertion began to weaken us. That night a cold misting rain peppered our perch on the side of a ledge. By morning, we were desperate for food. We decided to take a chance at going back down to the coastal road on the western shore. We cautiously hedged downhill in search for something to eat. We found a banana plantation, but the bananas were not yet ripe. They were about the size of a piece of chalk—and less tasty, but we each ate a couple and moved on up the road. By mid-morning we stumbled into an area that previously had been an army camp. There were clothing of all kinds, rifles, ammunition, and bolo knives, but no food!

Hungry and hunted men can become irrational. Even common events bulge out of proportion. Sounds become alarm bells. Panic borders every event. We were in that condition when a rustling in the bushes sent chills through our skinny bodies. With wide eyes we looked up to see a skinny old horse ambling toward us—food at last! Bill immediately proposed that we shoot the horse and cut off a couple of steaks. We shot him and sliced off several generous steaks for ourselves. We were so engrossed in our efforts that we failed to give any thought to the Japanese. We were busy trying to build a fire when three shots came ringing through the jungle.

We dropped everything and like a couple of scared rabbits dived into the jungle. Sure that we were being pursued, we clawed, scratched, and ripped through the jungle until we were breathless and totally exhausted. We stopped and threw ourselves into a clump of bushes. There we waited and listened for a sound of our pursuers. We remained hidden for the rest of the day, all night, and all the next day.

As darkness again fell, we quietly made our way down to the coastal road and headed to the north toward Subic Bay. By this time, we were so exhausted that we could walk only one kilometer at a time. Then we would drop to the ground to revive our strength.

The next morning, we found a cashew tree with delicious cashew fruit. It was the first real food we had partaken since our dinner with the Filipinos four days previously. Later that day, in the town of Moron, another family provided us with a beautiful meal of Filipino food.

We waited until dark, then walked along the hilly trail until we reached Subic Bay. There, we were distressed to learn that the Japanese had commandeered or destroyed all boats suitable for a trip across the China Sea. Therefore, we changed our plans and began looking for a suitable craft for sailing to Australia more than 2,000 miles away.

Our ill-fated journey came to a sudden halt some days later when Bill Harris and I became separated. I found a couple of mining engineers with a boat ready to sail to Australia. They invited me to join them, but our sailing trip ended abruptly.

We were captured by a group of hostile Filipinos. They tied our hands behind us with a rope from our own boat. Then we were escorted by armed guard with drawn weapons to the local civilian jail. Our captors explained that they were turning us over to the Japanese for our own protection. It was not the kind of protection we were looking for, but we had no choice.

We were transported to Manila and lodged in a dungeon in ancient Spanish Fort Santiago. My new companions were Ralph Conrad of Oakland, California, and Frank Bacon from El Paso, Texas. They were mining engineers who had wandered from Baguio in the northern part of Luzon to the southern end of the island. When we were captured, I also claimed to be from the mines in Baguio. I told the Japanese that my name was Robert Fred Johnson and that I was the son of a mine superintendent in Baguio. I knew that torture and death awaited me if I disclosed that I was an escaped US Air Corps officer.

The three of us were lodged in separate cells so that we had no opportunity to communicate. All I had was a name and a city. I desperately needed more information about the real Robert Johnson if I were to impersonate him.

Soon the Japanese moved me. A big wooden door swung open and I was pushed into a wooden cage approximately 12 feet by 12 feet. The room seemed large enough except that there were already 12 people in it!

In one of the rear corners was a water spigot in a box at about floor level so that by resting on my hands and knees I could get a drink of water. In the other rear corner was a hole in the floor with a bucket below it to be used as a toilet.

From the middle of the ceiling hung a lightbulb (of approximately 25 watts) that was illuminated night and day. On the wall in three languages were the house rules.

1. We were not to talk to one another.
2. During the daytime we were to sit with our back to the wall.
3. At night we were to lie on the floor to sleep.

There were no bunks or pillows or covers. We had the hard floor for a bed.

By whispering, we learned about each other: Roy C. Bennett, an American, the former editor of the *Manila Daily Bulletin*;

McCullough Dick, the former editor of the *Manila Times*; two Frenchmen who were said to be members of a Free French Organization; several Filipinos; and one Chinese boy.

Three of the walls were of plywood construction; but the front of the cell was made of three-inch by three-inch wooden bars placed about one-half inch apart. In the center of the front of the cell was a small opening about four feet above the floor. This was a serving window where, three times a day, a little Japanese soldier appeared with a bucket and generously rationed each of us with a heaping saucer of rice. Sometimes he would put some green leaves on the rice. Other times there would be bony pieces of fish. On Sundays and Thursdays, we got a special treat when, instead of the rice, we got a saucer of milk with some sugar and a small cube of bread. No other food was served to us at anytime. No utensils were provided. The skinny bodies lined up before the serving window. They grabbed their saucer and ran back to sit on the floor and gobble up their rice, pushing it in their mouths with their fingers.

The monotony of our routine was broken several times each day and night by roll call. We could hear it start at the other end of the row, 13 cells away from us. When we heard the command, "Ro Co!" we each jumped up and stood facing the front of the cell. Then, when the guard appeared before our cell, we would count off in Japanese. Bennett, my American friend, prompted me so I would say the correct number.

So, for about a half-hour at each roll call, we would hear ringing up and down the halls outside, "ichi, ne, san, shi, go, roku, hichi, hachi, ku, ju, ju-ne, ju-san, etc." Sometimes there would be no roll call for three or four hours, then we might have one followed by another and then another. There seemed to be no rhyme nor reason to the way it was done.

From Bennett I learned that the people in the cell had each been arrested by the military police. The Japanese practice was to go to the home of the person in the middle of the night. If the one who answered the door was the person they wanted, he would be taken immediately, with no opportunity to communicate with members of his family. For that reason, many of the prisoners wore very few clothes. Bennett himself wore only a pair of BVDs, the only clothing he had for several months.

From time to time, the guard would appear at the front of the cell and call the name of an individual prisoner. The big wooden door would be opened and the prisoner would be taken away. Sometimes they would return to the cell badly beaten and lie on the floor in a heap, moaning and groaning until they were sufficiently revived to sit along the wall.

Sometimes a prisoner would go for interrogation and never return to the cell. Authorities estimated after the war that only one of 10 people who entered Fort Santiago came out alive.

My concern that I might be taken out for questioning was short-lived. I heard the guard calling a name, but it meant nothing to me. Bennett nudged me and beckoned for me to stand in front of the window. The guard was calling, "Roberto Johnson"—my new name.

The door opened. I stepped down out of the cell and put on my shoes to follow the little guard down the long corridor. We passed the cells of Ralph and Frank, whom I had not seen for several days. With the little guard, I hiked across the inner court of Fort Santiago to a room in another building.

There was a table, three chairs, an officer, and an interpreter. In the corner stood a wooden pick handle and a piece of pipe about three feet long and about three-fourths of an inch thick. The officer spoke in Japanese and the interpreter translated his questions into English. Each question and each answer were written on a scroll.

I gave my name as Robert Fred Johnson and said that I was the son of the superintendent of Le Panto Mine near Baguio. I was from Miami, Arizona, and I had come to the Philippines on a ship before the war to work at the mine with my father.

Because I was an escaped prisoner of war, I knew I could not say anything that would identify me with the military. I was a soldier in civilian clothes in enemy territory. Had they known of my flight to the Philippines with the B-17s or of my activities on Bataan or Corregidor, I would have been executed.

After a long session of questioning, I was taken back to my cell. After that first session, I was called for questioning each day. The officer started each session from the beginning and asked all of the same questions that he had asked the day before.

I told of how Bacon, Conrad, and I had left the mine at the outbreak of war and spent eight months walking south. It was more than 200 miles from Baguio to the south coast, where our trip ended. Questioning went well for me until the interpreter started finding fault with my story. My answers to the questions were not the same as the answers of my comrades. It became very difficult. If only I could talk with my friends, I could get the right answers. The problem was that they were in separate cells and there was no way to communicate.

After a few days, my questioning period was interrupted when I fell sick with malaria. I lay on the hard floor with fever, racked with pain, asking for a doctor. Each time the Japanese response was, "By and by the doctor come." However, the doctor never came.

When I had recovered enough to sit up, I was again taken for questioning. The officer's attitude was different now. He was very genial. He pulled out a package of American Lucky Strike cigarettes and offered me one. My first thought was that the cigarettes had come from Red Cross packages intended for the prisoners. I took one and inhaled deeply. The Japanese officer said, "You tell the truth—it is very good for you. You lie and you will be killed. Yesterday you lie. Today you lie, you will be killed." The session ended, and I was taken back to my cell.

When I was taken for questioning the next day, the officer flew into a rage as I stepped into the room. It was all in Japanese, but the interpreter let me know that I was not fit to sit on a chair. I must get on my knees on the floor. The officer raged on, and pointed to the pipe in the corner. The interpreter handed it to him and he struck me across the back time and again. After the first couple of blows, I was numb and felt only dull thuds as the pipe struck my body.

I was then taken back to my cell where I felt like dropping to the floor as I had seen others do. Instead I made my way over to the wall and sat beside Bennett. I did not have to tell him what had happened. He knew. The next day I was on the floor again with malaria, but there was still no doctor.

When I was returned for questioning a few days later, the session went on and on into the night. "You tell the truth, it is very good for you. You can go to Santo Tomas Internment Camp with your friends. It is very nice. You lie, you will be killed."

Then came questions about a town called Lusud where Ralph and Frank had spent some time. My description of the place was not satisfactory. Finally, the officer produced a paper and asked me to draw a map. I did it. I drew a map of a typical Filipino barrio but I could not please the officer. He tore up the paper and threw it to the floor.

It was near midnight after about six hours of gruelling questioning when he gave me a paper and pencil and told me to take them back to my cell. I was to have a proper map of the town of Lusud when I came for questioning again.

With a heavy heart, I followed the guard back across the courtyard and down the long corridor past the cells of sleeping prisoners. As I leaned over to remove my shoes, I looked up to see the guard unlocking the wrong cell. I started to blurt out, "Wrong cell," but I remained silent. The guard was unlocking the cell of my friend, Ralph Conrad. I could not believe it as the big door swung open and I stepped in. I held my breath while the door slammed behind me, and the bolt was jammed into its place.

I climbed over the bodies stretched out on the floor to my friend, Ralph. He had been asleep and he seemed bewildered by my presence in his cell. I crowded in beside him on the floor and related my plight. Quickly, and quietly as possible, I asked him questions and had him draw my map. We needed to act quickly before the guard learned of his mistake. Fortunately, the guard did not return and we had a long session. Then I called the guard to report the mistake. By this time, a new guard was on duty and he did not understand.

Now outside the cell, I pointed to the name tags by the door to my cell. They were in Japanese, but I assumed one of them said Robert Johnson. Ignoring my efforts to explain, he reached out his hand and demanded that I give him my map. I refused and, unbelievably, he let me keep it. He then locked me in my own cell. Following those nervous moments, there came two roll calls in succession. Then all was quiet. I lay on the floor pondering over the events of the past few hours. I could not believe what had happened.

The next day, I presented my map to the officer when I was taken for questioning. He was satisfied and I felt as if I had passed the most important test of my life. I had the right answers for the officer's questions for a couple of succeeding sessions before getting into trouble again. There seemed to be no way out and I was worried. I did not know the answers to the questions, and I had no way to talk to either of my companions.

Then, one morning when I was called, I stepped out of my cell to see the haggard figures of my two companions, Bacon and Conrad. They were also out of their cells. I was certain we were being taken out for execution. I could tell they were worried too. We were led across the courtyard without a word between us to a different building. Then the guard took each of us inside one at a time. I was shown a map and asked to point out the route we had travelled for the past eight months. I did the best I could and was taken out to join the other two. Then the guard loaded us into a military staff car, and we were driven out of the gate of Fort Santiago. We rode on across Manila for about a mile and through a big gate into a compound. There we saw hundreds of American and British people. They looked at us curiously as we unloaded from the staff car. Much to our surprise and delight, we learned that we had arrived at the Santo Tomas Civilian Internment Camp.

Deliverance

Carl Mydans was one of the original photographers employed by *Life* magazine when it first brought to the American scene a pictorial review of world news. He covered the Russian invasion of Finland in the frigid winter of 1940 with pictures of a war unlike any that had been witnessed before. Then he and his pretty wife, Shelley, were transferred to Chungking to cover the Japanese war in China.

The year of 1941 found Carl and Shelley in the Philippine Islands reporting the tragic plight of the Americans after the attack by the Japanese. In the early days of that war, the editor of *Life* had requested a story about Americans on the offensive. Shelley's reply had been short and to the point: "Bitterly regret your request unavailable here," she reported.

It was true. The American forces were suffering defeat at every turn. Manila was declared an open city, but that did not deter the Japanese from continuing their bombing attacks on the city. Within days, the Mydans found themselves interned with 3,500 other Americans, British, and Dutch in Santo Tomas University. The stately complex within the city of Manila would be the residence of most of the civilians for the duration of the war.

The war had gone much better for the Japanese than they had anticipated. Within six months after the war began, they faced the problem of providing food and shelter for a tremendous number of prisoners of war and civilian internees. Included were the 80,000 prisoners from Corregidor and Bataan, together with 3,700 civilian internees in Santo Tomas and Baguio.

Many of the Santo Tomas internees desired to be moved to Shanghai, where they had relatives and friends. But there was no internment in Shanghai, so the civilians would have to provide their own food and shelter. The Japanese officials determined that such a move would be to their own benefit. Such a move would help solve the food shortage in the Philippines.

Carl and Shelley Mydans applied for transfer to Shanghai, along with 42 other Americans and a number of Dutch and British. I, too, applied for transfer to Shanghai. On my first evening in Santo Tomas Internment Camp, I had gone to the barber for a haircut. Somebody there mentioned that a number of internees were being transferred to Shanghai. It was the first time I had heard anything about it. That started me thinking and asking questions. My head started to swim. Could it be possible that I might get on that ship, too? I could not believe it. It seemed totally unreal to me that the Japanese would transfer me to China. China had been our destination when Bill Harris and I had escaped from Corregidor more than four months before. I thought about what a strange thing it would be if I could get to China after all of the difficulties we had endured over those past four months. I decided to give it a try.

The next morning, as soon as I thought he would be in his office, I went to see the commandant. I introduced myself as Robert Fred Johnson, a mine employee from the area of Baguio and told him that I had been wandering about the islands since the beginning of the war. I told him that I had arrived in camp and had learned about the trip just the day before. I also told him that I wanted to be transferred to Shanghai, where I had relatives and friends.

"I am sorry, Mr Johnson," the commandant replied tersely. "The list has been made up. There will be no names added and no names taken off the list."

That seemed final enough, but I made one more try before I left his office. "If there is any chance that my name could be added to the list, I would surely appreciate it," I pleaded.

The wild dream had faded. I had tried and failed. Somehow I knew that it could not happen that easily, so I gave up the idea of getting on the ship to Shanghai and spent the next few days trying to find a way to escape over the wall of the internment camp.

I was housed in a big gymnasium with a camp cot, a mosquito net, sheets, and a pillow. The internees wore clean clothes and ate their meals at tables, with plates, knives, forks, and spoons. Those were luxuries that I had not enjoyed for months. I took the job of washing pots and pans in the kitchen and, in general, found life relatively enjoyable. With it all, however, I knew that I had to get away from that place before my identity became known. There were many people in camp from the Baguio mines, and they all knew that I had nothing to do with the mines. There was no doubt in my mind that I would be executed if the Japanese learned the truth about me.

Before I was able to work out a way to escape, a miraculous thing happened. The sailing list was posted and the name of Robert Fred Johnson was among the people who would be transferred to Shanghai. It was as if I were in a dream world. I, a lieutenant in the United States Army Air Corps, was being assisted by the Japanese in my escape from their prison camp, and I was being transported on a Japanese ship to Shanghai.

Within 10 days from the time I had arrived in Santo Tomas, I was on the way. We went first by bus to the port, then boarded the *Maya Maru* for Shanghai. Things had happened so quickly that I was having a hard time putting my thoughts together.

During the past few days I had been obsessed with escape, and the Japanese had solved that problem for me. Now I faced an equally perplexing problem. In the event I reached Shanghai, how could I make my way across 1,343 miles of China to Chungking? When I had been with Bill Harris, that had not seemed such a problem. Bill had been stationed in Shanghai with the Fourth Marine Regiment and was acquainted with the countryside. I knew nothing about China and had no idea of what to do.

I needed to talk to somebody who could help me—somebody I could trust. I learned about Carl and Shelley Mydans, and decided to try to get their help. I saw them and watched them. I wondered how I might be able to get acquainted with them, and how much I could say about myself. Late on the first day of the trip, I saw them on deck. It was just as our ship was passing through the north channel between Corregidor and Bataan. Suddenly, on impulse, I found myself saying to them: "There's old Cabcaben Field." The Mydans turned to me and Mr Mydans said sharply, "That's not the kind of talk to have on this ship."

Embarrassed, I left them. I worried about what had happened but I desperately needed help. I found them again when they were alone. "I'm sorry about what I said," I told them. "I know how unwise I was to have said it. But I need to talk to someone and I need help."

Carl Mydans said, "Alright! If you will give us your word that you will not tell anyone else about your background—not a single soul—we'll do all we can to help you."

The day after our conversation I suffered a relapse of malaria fever. The disease had plagued me from the days in the jungles of Bataan. I was confined to my cot in the hold of the ship for several days, unable to move about. At long last, the *Maya Maru* made its way into the Yangtze estuary and up the Huangpu River to the Bund on the Shanghai waterfront. It was night when we arrived, and we were unceremoniously unloaded from the ship. Friends and relatives enjoyed tearful reunions, laughing and crying all around us. Faithful Chinese friends came with great joy as people rushed to get back to their Shanghai homes.

I watched and waited, and then was bewildered when I came to the realization that I was free to go wherever I wanted to go. The problem was that I did not have any place to go. There was no one to talk to. Then I heard someone shout, "Transportation to the American School. Transportation to the American School." That sounded good to me. Some people were climbing on board a truck with their belongings, so I joined them. My only worldly possessions at the time were the clothes I was wearing—a sport shirt, a pair of trousers, and a pair of tennis shoes. I was delighted to learn that an American Association of Shanghai assisted people who were in need of help. The organization had provided the truck to haul homeless passengers to the American School in the French Quarter of the city. In addition to the transportation, there was food and a place to sleep. It was comfortable, clean, and quiet—and a long way from the horrible scenes of Bataan, Corregidor, Fort Santiago, and that wall that had surrounded Santo Tomas.

I did not see the Mydans for several days after we landed in Shanghai. I wanted desperately to see them and talk with them, but I did not know where they were and did not know how to find them. Then, one day, they appeared at the American School library where they had come to get reading material. When the opportunity came, I asked when I could talk with them. They told me they were staying at the Palace Hotel on the Bund and I could come to see them at any time. The next day I took the street car into the business area of the city and went nervously knocking on their door. This would be the first time I could tell anyone about my problems.

I started first by telling them that I was a navigator in the US Army Air Corps. With that, Carl indicated that we should move to the middle of the room where the three of us sat on the floor while I quietly told them of the past nine months. I explained that I wanted to get to Chungking and back to my outfit in the South Pacific.

Carl said, "The government has spent a lot of money training you. The best thing for you to do is talk to Anker B. Henningsen. He works with the American Association here in Shanghai. He is reliable and you can trust him." I was greatly relieved. I now had friends with whom I could share my worries and my plans. I felt much better after my visit with the Mydans.

When I made my way to Henningsen's office, a new fear gripped me. Sitting at the reception desk in the hall was an oriental gentleman who looked very Japanese to me. I decided that I would tell Henningsen nothing until I learned why he had a Japanese for a receptionist. I was blunt and came straight to the point. "Who is that fellow sitting outside your office?" I inquired.

"Oh," Henningsen laughed. "That is Peter Kim. He is Korean and he hates the Japanese just as much as we do. Don't worry about him. What can I do for you?"

I told him my story and of my desire to go to Chungking. He looked worried and warned me sternly. He told me of six US Marines who had attempted to escape from Shanghai and make their way back to Chungking. Their effort had ended in disaster even though some of them could speak Chinese and knew the territory well. The Japanese captured them and lodged them in the Bridge House Prison. That was the Shanghai counterpart of Fort Santiago in Manila, where I had been held and beaten by the Japanese.

Before I departed, Henningsen noticed the clothes I was wearing. He asked me if I had any others. I let him know that the clothes on my back represented my entire wardrobe. With that, he said, "Lets take a walk."

We went down to the street on the elevator. It took a lively step to keep stride with him as we wound our way through streets and alleys until we arrived at his downtown apartment. He opened a wardrobe and took out a fine Hart, Schaffner & Marks suit.

"Here, try this on," he said as he handed it to me. It fit me perfectly. Then there was a shirt, a tie, and a pair of Florshiem shoes which were also my exact size. I felt like a new person, and I was very grateful to the generous gentleman. Back at the American School, the disappointing news about chances to escape from Shanghai mellowed as I enjoyed a new feeling of respectability in my new attire.

The Japanese required all American citizens to wear a red arm band with a large letter "A" with a number. British citizens' arm bands bore a "B." My number happened to be 1215 which provided a constant reminder of the approximate time of day that the Japanese had carried out their devastating raid against Clark Field back in the Philippines. In addition to the arm bands, we were provided individual identification cards with our picture and a message explaining our status as enemy aliens (fig. 4). There were no other restrictions upon us. We were able to travel freely about the fascinating oriental city of Shanghai.

Just when I felt comfortably settled into my new surroundings, a disconcerting thing happened. I was summoned to the Swiss Consulate in downtown Shanghai to answer questions about my identity. As a neutral nation, the Swiss had the responsibility of taking care of matters concerning the Americans in China. I was told that they were unable to confirm my American citizenship. I had no passport or any other identification. In Fort Santiago, I had told the Japanese that my parents, Fred and Betty Johnson, lived in Miami, Arizona. US State Department people were unable to locate anyone by that name in Miami, Arizona. I was in trouble.

At that time I had to confess that my middle name was Doud. I told the Swiss that my father, Fred Johnson, had been disappointed that I had not been named after him, so I had adopted his name as my middle name.

"I have a sister named Laura Showalter living in Columbus, Indiana, who can identify me as Robert Doud Johnson," I told the Swiss counsel. The message was sent through Berne, Switzerland, to the US State Department. My citizenship was confirmed, and I was issued an identification card by the Swiss Consulate Embassy.

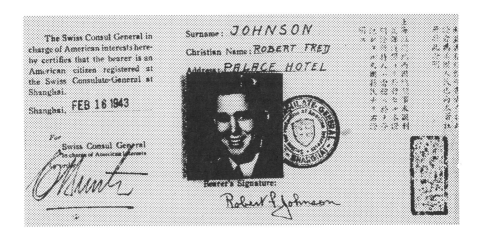

The Swiss Consul General in charge of American interests hereby certifies that the bearer is an American citizen registered at the Swiss Consulate-General at Shanghai.

Shanghai, FEB 16 1943

For
Swiss Consul General

Surname: JOHNSON
Christian Name: ROBERT FRED
Address: PALACE HOTEL

Bearer's Signature:
Robert F Johnson

Figure 4. Author's Identification as Civilian Internee

Life in my new environment was pleasant beyond all expectations. I made friends and attended parties. There were horse races at a splendid race course on Nanking Road. I learned years later that some members of the American community in Shanghai had been suspicious of me. The expression was that I was "unknown," a person with no passport or credible identification.

My activities came to an abrupt end when I was stricken with a recurrence of malaria fever. Dr Hyla S. Watters, the missionary doctor at the American School, became alarmed at my condition. She said that it was malignant malaria and could be fatal. Dr Watters, a longtime medical missionary in China, gave me a stringent prescription. She had studied tropical diseases in London and she knew of a possible cure. If I would consent, she would give me a shot of salvarsan, a medicine used on syphilis patients. After lying in bed for days with fever and misery, I was willing to try anything. She administered the medicine. The results were phenomenal. In a few days, the fever was gone—and I never had a recurrence of the dreaded disease.

The Mydans continued to stop by the American School from time to time to renew their stock of reading material. On one such visit, they suggested that I might enjoy moving to the Palace Hotel on the Bund where they lived. What was more, they offered to provide me with money to make the move possible. In a short time, I was living in a private room at the hotel with a fireplace and a view up the Huangpu River from the front window. It was cozy and comfortable. Evenings, the local radio station XMHA played its sweet theme song at sign-off time. Sometimes, in moments of deep nostalgia, I would gaze out the window and wonder if someday I might be sailing out that river and back home to America. But it seemed very much like an impossible dream.

On a cold and dreary November morning in 1942, the American and British communities were shocked to learn that a number of the leading members of their community had been interned. Among them was Anker B. Henningsen. They were confined in Potung, a compound across the Huangpu River. There were rumors that more would be taken. Then, in late January, it became official. All American, British, and Dutch citizens in Shanghai were to be interned. Those of us who had come from Manila had enjoyed five months of semifreedom in a phenomenal, enchanting, and mysterious city known as "The Pearl of the Orient." We were ordered to report to the Columbia Country Club on 3 February 1943 to be assigned to an internment camp. From there, we moved to a war-torn and abandoned Chinese university on the outskirts of the city. It came to be known as Chapei Internment Camp.

The grounds at Chapei were some five acres, with few trees and little shrubbery. I was again living in a compound surrounded by barbed wire. I looked longingly at the broad, open fields to the west and wondered if it might be possible to escape. How could I get away and make it over the 1,343 miles to Chungking? As far as I knew, I was the only military person in the Shanghai internment camp, which housed about 1,000 American, British, and Dutch civilian internees. I would have to do all of the planning myself.

As I was pondering over the problem of how I might escape, I would have been surprised to learn that one of my former classmates was also working on an escape plan. He was

Harold Fulghum, a lanky, hazel-eyed lad from Quinlan, Texas. But he was not in the Far East. He was a prisoner of the Germans halfway around the world in a camp known as Stalag III. He had graduated from Texas Tech with a BS degree in chemistry before the war. Harold had been on his seventh mission, bombing German submarine pens at Saint Nazaire along the French coast when his B-17 was hit by antiaircraft fire. He suffered a broken jaw, and pieces of flak in his left leg and hip, before he bailed out of the plane. He was in the water and unconscious when the Germans picked him up and hauled him off to spend the remaining 33 months of the war in a military prisoner of war camp with 15,000 American and British flyers.

Fulghum and about 800 others were engaged in a project that was to become known as "The Great Escape." It was reputed to be the most ingenious escape effort in the history of warfare. The project taxed the cunning of the American and British flyers to the utmost. The finished product of their efforts was a tunnel 35 feet deep and 500 feet long. Of the 800 involved in the project, only 200 prisoners were selected for a nighttime effort to escape. Seventy-six prisoners were able to work their way through the long tunnel before they were spotted by German guards. Seventy-two of the 76 were captured, and 50 were shot in cold blood. Only four were able to reach England safely.

Fulghum was not among the escapees. He had been denied the opportunity to escape. His regularly assigned duty in camp was in the food store, but for escape purposes he was assigned to the security detail under American Capt Albert ("Junior") P. Clark (later Lt Gen A. P. Clark). Near the end of the war, Fulghum was moved to a camp north of Munich. In a dramatic move, General Patton's 14th Armored Division surrounded the camp and rescued the prisoners. Harold Fulgham remained in the military service until he retired on 31 October 1960.

A thousand men, women, and children crowded into former classrooms at Chapei Internment Camp. I shared a rather large room with 14 other men. There were bunks with rectangular, box-type mosquito nets covering each one. There was no room for furniture other than a chest for personal belongings placed at the foot of each bunk.

175

Carl Mydans occupied another dormitory-style room down the hall in the same building. Shelley spent a lot of time out of camp for medical treatment because Japanese and German doctors confirmed that she was losing the sight in one of her eyes.

As always, there was the persistent rumor of repatriation for the internees. There had been one previous exchange of civilians from Shanghai and, even though it occurred early in the war, it was plausible that there might be another. The rumors did not excite me because I was certain that I would be among the last to go even if there were another repatriation. I was more concerned about the possibility of getting through that barbed wire fence and to Chungking. I had no passport or other citizenship papers. There was only the identification card which the Swiss had furnished. One thing was certain, I did not want the Japanese officials to start asking questions about my identity.

One evening when Carl and I were talking, he hinted that I might have a chance to be repatriated. Because of my special circumstances, a request had been made to the US State Department. The request was that all people who had come from Manila to Shanghai be repatriated in a block. That would include me if my real identity had not been exposed before that time. Repatriation seemed to be developing into a sure thing, and excitement grew in camp as we were waiting for the list to be posted. It was then that the unexpected happened.

After long, anxious days, the list was finally published on the bulletin board amidst much excitement. Carl, with a broad smile across his face, announced, "You're there!" I was shocked! It was beyond belief. I looked at the list and read the name, "Robert F. Johnson." It could not be true, but there it was. I was going home. Yet I could not think of home. It was in another world. Too many things could happen. So many things had already happened that I was afraid to think this was real.

Carl and Shelley Mydans were there by my side. They had put their own security in jeopardy to help a fellow they knew needed help. I knew that they had succeeded when I stepped off the exchange ship *Grisholm* in New York Harbor on 8 December 1943, free to go back to my unit in the Air Corps.

A Visit with Charlie

The Pan American Navigation School at Coral Gables closed unceremoniously in October 1944, almost a year before the end of WWII. The cadets had gone and the University of Miami was back to normal as if the cadets had never been there. All that remained of the navigation school was in the minds and memories of those who had been part of it. Officials of the Army Air Corps decided that the old Sikorsky and Consolidated flying boats had outlived their usefulness as navigation training planes. They said that they were too slow, there were not enough of them, and they did not afford an adequate amount of overland training, a requisite for Air Corps navigators. The truth was that the Air Corps had in-service schools geared to meet all of the needs of the military for the duration of the war. The Pan American School was no longer needed, and Charlie Lunn accepted a position as superintendent of Ground Training for Pan American Airways at Miami.

One afternoon after work, I stopped in for a visit with him and his wife Sylvia at their modest cottage at 261 N. W. 62d Court, near the Miami International Airport. Sylvia answered the door and called Charlie from the backyard where he was grilling steaks for dinner.

"Well, Whit, it has been a long time!" he exclaimed excitedly. He threw his arms around me and greeted me like a father greeting a long-lost son coming home from the wars. When the steaks were finished, the three of us sat at the dining room table to reminisce about days gone by. He asked about where I had been and what I had been doing since the war. But Charlie was an entirely different man from the Charlie I had known as the guru of navigational knowledge. He was no longer the lecturer, the imparter of knowledge. He wanted to visit and talk about "his boys." He told me about the exciting things that had happened at the school. In addition to the American cadets, he had trained cadets from many other countries, including Brazil, China, Columbia, New Zealand,

and England. Charlie also talked about his earlier years at Key West where he had been friends with Ernest Hemingway. Then Sylvia proudly displayed a copy of a manuscript she had typed for the great author.

Charlie related how he happened to pilot Hemingway's new 38-foot fishing boat, the *Pilar*, from Key West to Havana. Ernest had hurried down to Joe Russell's bar on Green Street (later one of Key West's favorite watering holes, known as Sloppy Joe's) to see if Joe would pilot his new boat to Havana. Joe could not make the trip because the bar was full of sailors off a destroyer in the harbor. When Hemingway turned to Captain Lunn, Charlie was happy to pilot the *Pilar* to Havana for him.

"I've got a better one than that," Charlie said enthusiastically. "We were visited by a king."

"A king?" I asked. "Who was that?"

Then Charlie related that in September 1941 former King Edward VIII of England had made a secret visit to Coral Gables to review the British Royal Air Force cadets in training under Charlie. He was the king who had abdicated his throne to marry American divorcée Wallis Warfield Simpson. As governor of the Bahamas, his visit was an expression of gratitude from the British government to the US for training 1,224 much-needed aerial navigators for the British Royal Air Force.

I knew that it had been an exciting life for Charlie Lunn, coming from Key West as a high school dropout. He became a ship's captain and, later, chief instructor for the country's first class of military aerial navigators.

As we sat there in his dining room that evening, I could tell that his greatest delight in life had to do with the accomplishments of "his boys." To him, we were more important than piloting the fishing boat for Ernest Hemingway or even meeting a former king of England.

My mind went back to a beautiful moonlight night at our graduation party at the Coral Gables Country Club. To show our gratitude to Charlie for teaching us celestial navigation, we had presented him with an expensive gold watch. In acknowledging the gift, Charlie stood before his admiring cadets. He blurted out a few words in trying to tell us what it had all meant to him. Then tears welled up in his eyes as he said, "Oh, hell, fellows, you know how I feel." That was the beginning and ending of his speech. We did know exactly how he felt.

Throughout the war, few of us had known the fate of other cadets. We were scattered about the globe with only an occasional meeting of former classmates. One thing we all had in common was an adoration for Charles J. Lunn. He had prepared us for the new world in which we lived. He had given us confidence to fly the uncharted seas around the world. Though it had been more than four years since the graduation of that first class, Charlie spoke of my classmates as if they were members of his own family. He was especially proud of Ted Boselli and Walter Seamon, who had served as navigators on the first presidential planes for President Roosevelt and President Truman. He was also proud that Leo George Clarke, Jr., another of his star students, had served as the chief navigation briefing officer for the Bolero Project that moved the Eighth Air Force from the US to the United Kingdom. He had followed our careers and maintained a bulletin board on which he recorded our achievements.

The board showed the scores of military honors which had been awarded to the former cadets by the government. It also reflected the tragedies that had befallen so many of the cadets. It recorded the tragedies of Robert L. Brown and John J. Kiyak, killed on training missions as navigation instructors. Brown had been the first member of our class to be lost back in the summer of 1941. It also recorded the loss of Moslener at Hickam Field on the first day of the war by the first bomb. Then there had been the loss of Richard Cease at McKassar Strait, William Meenagh over northern Australia, Francis Rang at Messina, Italy, and Jay Horowitz off the coast of China. These were all very personal losses to our old navigation instructor.

Charlie's impact upon navigational training in the military was immense. Eight cadets from his first class took assignments in newly established Air Corps schools scattered about the United States. They were: John B. Armstrong and Norman P. Hays at Randolph Field, Texas; John J. Kiyak and Roger H. Terzian at Maxwell Field, Alabama; Robert W. Snyder, Jr., and Carl L. Steig at Barksdale Field, Louisiana; and Clarence R. Winter and Robert L. Brown at Moffett Field, California.

They taught techniques and procedures which they had learned from Charlie Lunn. In addition, the US Navy had sent several classes of cadets to the Pan American School at Coral Gables. They then assigned their outstanding graduates from his school as instructors in celestial navigation.

In the following years during WWII, the US Air Corps trained more than 50,000 celestial navigators. The roots of the entire program reached back to the "Cardboard College" in Coral Gables, where Charlie Lunn had labored so diligently to make his cadets understand the intricate details of celestial navigation. Thus it might be possible that Charles J. Lunn influenced the techniques and procedures of more US navigators than any person in history.

But for all his contribution to the war effort, he received no notoriety, no awards, no decorations of any kind from the US government during his lifetime. But notoriety was not what he wanted. What he did want was for his cadets to learn celestial navigation and learn it well.

The University of Miami bestowed upon the high school dropout an unprecedented degree: doctor of navigation. That he was, with a brilliant mind and a mastery of the subject, which he had learned through self-study. Upon his death on 30 March 1983, Sylvia received a routine certificate from the United States of America honoring the memory of Charles J. Lunn:

> This certificate is awarded by a grateful nation in recognition of devoted and selfless consecration in the service of our country in the Armed Forces of the United States.
>
> s/ Ronald Reagan
> President of the United States.[1]

It was merely a routine acknowledgement from the government as sent to all families of deceased service members. Only Sylvia Lunn and those flyers who had charted routes where man had never flown before could understand the extent of devotion and selfless consecration that Charles J. Lunn had given for his country.

Notes

1. Office of the President, Certificate, 1983, mailgram provided by Sylvia Lunn to author.

Appendix A

History

A training program for navigators in the military was not a spur of the moment decision.* The need for such training was suggested as early as 1923 by Lt Albert F. Hagenberger, Army Air Service. In the beginning, learning to fly simply meant to take off, fly about the countryside, and then land the plane safely. After that came cross-country trips which entailed flying from point A to point B. Such trips could be accomplished in clear weather with minimal training and preparation. When problems arose, early flyers would resort to a navigational aid commonly known as "the iron compass." In layman's language that meant following the railroad tracks to your destination. Adverse weather created difficult navigational obstacles which would require navigational instruments and training in procedures not yet developed in the early 1920s.

Lieutenant Hagenberger, who had completed a special one-year course in aeronautical engineering at MIT in 1919, recognized deeper needs for training. In 1923 he submitted a report entitled, "The Importance of Developing Aerial Navigation Instruments and Methods to the Army Air Service." In his report he stated, "Some provisions must be made for training of personnel in their [aerial navigation instruments] use and for maintenance of instruments."[1] He also recommended that the tables of organization be revised to create the position of navigation officer.

Five years later a school was established at Wright Field, Dayton, Ohio, where for the first time in Army history, training was conducted with all available navigation instruments and equipment. Because of personnel problems, the school closed after one year. In that same year (1928), Lt B. R. Dallas sent a letter through channels to Army Air Corps General Headquarters (GHQ) stating,

---

*Unless otherwise noted, information in this appendix is from the Air Force Historical Foundation.

> there exists an important type of aerial operation for which there are no qualified personnel trained or in training, nor aircraft built or building capable of its successful operation. The mission involving these operations in searching at sea for and upon discovery, communicating the location of enemy invading forces.[2]

The office of Chief of Air Corps concurred in the recommendations and on 5 February 1932 steps were taken to establish an experimental unit. Harold Gatty, later famous as a navigator and around-the-world flyer, was employed as a civilian advisor in navigational matters and in development of special equipment. This was in line with Lieutenant Hagenberger's recommendations made nine years earlier, but this project, typical of many military programs, was discontinued after one month of operation. Mr Gatty was assigned to another project with a much higher military priority. It was a secret operation to be known as Frontier Defense Research Unit. His assistants were Capt Lawrence J. Carr, Lt Norris B. Harbold, and 10 airmen. In the following years, the Army Air Corps concentrated on the development and refinement of navigational procedures and equipment including drift meter, radio, octant, charts, and air almanacs.

Service testing of procedures and equipment developed by the Frontier Defense Research Unit was relegated to the 19th Bombardment Group, which had been activated in June 1932. Nine years later the 19th Group would be the first air group in combat in WWII using such procedures and equipment.

Between 1923 and 1940 navigation training programs were established at various US military fields including those at Wright, Rockwell, Langley, and Hawaii. In July 1936 a letter went out to all units listing the names of qualified navigators in General Headquarters Air Force. It identified 30 navigators qualified in celestial navigation and 61 qualified in dead reckoning navigation (navigating without the aid of celestial observations). By the spring of 1940, the Air Corps had only 80 experienced navigators, but it was well recognized that many, many more would be needed. No institution or combination of institutions was in being at that time which could produce navigators in quantities that would be needed in the event the United States should become involved in the war raging in Europe.

Gen Delos Emmons, chief of GHQ at the time, was a passenger on a Pan American clipper on a fact-finding mission to Europe when he became infatuated with work of the navigator, Charles Lunn. The general later contacted Pan American Airways and worked out a program for the company to provide instruction for navigation students at the University of Miami, Coral Gables, Florida.

Notes

1. Lt Albert Hagenberger, "The Importance of Developing Aerial Navigation Instruments and Methods to the Army Air Service" (McCook Field, Ohio: Instrument Section, 1 September 1923) in Lt Hagenberger's personal papers.

2. Norris B. Harbold, *The Log of Air Navigation* (San Antonio, Tex.: Naylor Co., 1970).

Appendix B

Class of 40-A

Name	Serial Number	Last Known Address
Albanese, Frederick T.	7031595	9044 E. Prairie Rd. Evanston, IL
Armstrong, John Bryant	0-409827	Unknown
Arnoldus, Robert Thermond	0-412133	La Grande, OR
Benes, Charles G.	7031597	2306 S. 59 Ave. Cicero, IL
Berkowitz, George Bernard	0-409896	2930 Peabody Dallas, TX
Boselli, Theodore John	0-377349	105 Audubon Ave. New York, NY
Brown, Robert Lawrence	0-409829	215 E. 11 Ave. Denver, CO
Cain, Carroll Joseph	0-409911	Ivesdale, IL
Cease, Richard Wellington	0-409912	17 Oak Ave. Trucksville, PA
Clarke, Leo George, Jr.	0-409897	c/o Maj L. G. Clarke Adj. Dept. Washington, DC
Cobb, Melvin Burdette	0-409913	Unknown
Cox, John Werner, Jr.	0-409898	1517 Central Ave. Great Falls, MT
Dawson, Paul Edward	0-409914	2331 W. 18th St. Wilmington, DE
Finnie, Thomas William	0-373698	535 Bramhall Ave. Jersey City, NJ
Gordon, Merrill Kern, Jr.	0-409910	Cascade, MT
Hays, Norman Pershing	0-408835	Tiff City, MO
Hoffman, Arthur Elkin	0-409899	144 N. Hamilton Dr. Beverley Hills, CA
Horowitz, Jay Malcom	0-409900	Sweetwater, TN

Name	Serial Number	Last Known Address
Jones, Jack Edward	0-409901	1302 West Avenue Austin, TX
Kiyak, John Joseph	0-408836	56 Compton Ave. Perth Amboy, NJ
Koterwas, Edmund A.	6998315	3639 Alabama Ave. S.E. Washington, DC
Markovich, George Michael	0-409903	2737 Magnolia Ave. Long Beach, CA
Marsh, Edward L.	6140506**	313 Wayne Ave. Lansdowne, PA
McAuliff, Harold Clayton	0-409902	658 Sacramento St. San Francisco, CA
*McCool, Harry	0-419329	LaJunta, CO
Meenagh, William Francis	0-372623	861 Cauldwell Ave. Bronx, NY
Moslener, Louis Gustav, Jr.	0-409917	356 12th St. Monaca, PA
Oliver, Anthony Edward	0-409904	38 Michigan Ave. Smithers, WV
Rang, Francis Bernard	0-409905	2868 Pearl St. Santa Monica, CA
Schreiber, Harry Julius	0-342127	2318 Avenue D Galveston, TX
Seamon, Walter Earle, Jr.	0-409906	West Jefferson, OH
Snyder, Robert Woodrow, Jr.	0-408837	3634 3rd Ave. San Diego, CA
Stevens, Charles John	0-409907	127 W. Montcalm Detroit, MI
Steig, Carl	0-382956	2023 29th St. Astoria, NY
Taylor, Homer Roy	0-409908	El Campo, TX
Tempest, Leroy T.	6587418**	Fairfield, WA

Name	Serial Number	Last Known Address
Terzian, Roger Hornsby	0-45833	328 S. Broadway Fresno, CA
Thompson, Berry Pershing	0-409918	Judith GAP, MT
Trenkle, Robert Anthony	0-395138	Le Roy, IL
Vifquain, Russell Manning	0-409919	524 Forest Glen Ames, IA
Walthers, George Arnold	0-409920	870 S. Race Denver, CO
Warner, William Scott	0-409909	Richlands, VA
Whitcomb, Edgar Doud	0-409910	Hayden, IN
*Wildner, Carl Richard	0-352857	Holyoke, MA
Wilson, James Franklin	0-409921	Ida, OK
Winter, Clarence Ralph	0-408834	Unknown

*Held over to graduate with succeeding class due to illness.

**Cadet serial numbers are used when other numbers are not available.

Bibliography

Army Air Forces. "Flying Training Command Historical Reviews." 1 January 1939–30 June 1946, held by Historical Research Agency, Maxwell AFB, Ala.

Baker, Carlos H. *Ernest Hemmingway: A Life Story.* New York: Scribner, 1969.

Belote, James H., and William H. Belote. *Corregidor: Saga of a Fortress.* New York: Harper & Row, 1967.

Boselli, Theodore J. Interview with Harris N. Done. California State College, Fullerton. Oral History Program. Community History Project. 27 April 1971.

Brown, Lt Col Charles M. *"The Oryoku Maru Story."* Magalia, Calif., 1983.

Chennault, Anna. *Chennault and the Flying Tigers.* New York: Paul S. Erickson, Inc., 1963.

Costello, John. *The Pacific War.* New York: Rawson, Wade, 1981.

Deering, Roscoe. *Presidential Aircraft.* Air Classics. Washington, D.C.

Glines, Carroll V. *The Doolittle Raid.* New York: Orion Books, 1988.

Godman, Col Henry C., and Cliff Dudley. *Supreme Commander.* Harrison, Ark.: New Leaf Press, 1980.

Gaff, Robert F. *Java 1942.* Buhl, Idaho: Thousand Springs Press, 1988.

Harbold, Norris B. *The Log of Air Navigation.* San Antonio, Tex.: Naylor Co., 1970.

Jones, D. Clayton. *The Years of MacArthur.* Boston, Mass.: Houghton Miffin, 1970.

Layton, Edwin T., Roger Pineau, and John Costello. *"And I Was There": Pearl Harbor and Midway—Breaking the Secrets.* New York: Morrow, 1985.

Lackie. *Deliver Us from Evil.* New York: Harper & Row, 1987.

LeMay, Curtis E., and Bill Yenne. *Superfortress—The B-29 and American Airpower.* New York: McGraw Hill, 1988.

Letter, 17 July 1990. Ref: 90/U 1024, JTR Alabama 36 112-6678. Headquarters USAF Historical Research Center, Maxwell AFB, Ala.

MacArthur, Douglas. *Reminiscences.* New York: McGraw-Hill, 1964.

Manchester, William R. *American Caesar, Douglas MacArthur, 1880–1964.* Boston: Little, Brown, and Co., 1978.

Memorandum to Chief Casualty Branch Ago No. 14430. 9 October 1947.

Montgomery, Gen Austin. "His Diary." 1945, held in General Montgomery's Papers, Alexandria, Va.

Mitchell, John H. *On Wings We Conquer.* Springfield, Mo.: GEM Publishers, 1990.

Okumira, Mastaka, Jiro Horikoshi, and Martin Caidin. *Zero— The Story of the Japanese Navy Air Force 1937–1945.* London: Transworld Publishers, Hunt, Bernard and Co., Ltd., 1958.

Owens, Frank. *The Fall of Singapore.* London: M. Joseph, 1960.

Pan American Airways, Inc. *New Horizons.* New York, December 1940, 11; August 1942, 17–18.

Spector, Ronald H. *Eagle Against the Sun.* The American War with Japan. New York: Free Press, 1985.

Thomas, Rowan T. *Born in Battle.* Philadelphia, Penn.: The John C. Winston Company, 1944.

"U.S. Army in World War II, The War in the Pacific, The Fall of the Philippines," in *Military History of the United States Army.* Edited by Louis Morton. Washington, D.C., 1953.

Vote, Robert. "The Death of Admiral Yamamoto." *The Retired Officer.* November 1979, 27–29.

War Department, Headquarters Army Air Forces. *Missing Air Crew Report*, No. 16453. Washington, D.C., 1943.

White, W. L. *Queens Die Proudly*. New York: Harcourt, Brace, and Company, 1943.

Wright, Monte Duane. *Most Probable Position: A History of Aerial Navigation to 1941*. Lawrence, Kans.: University Press of Kansas, 1972.

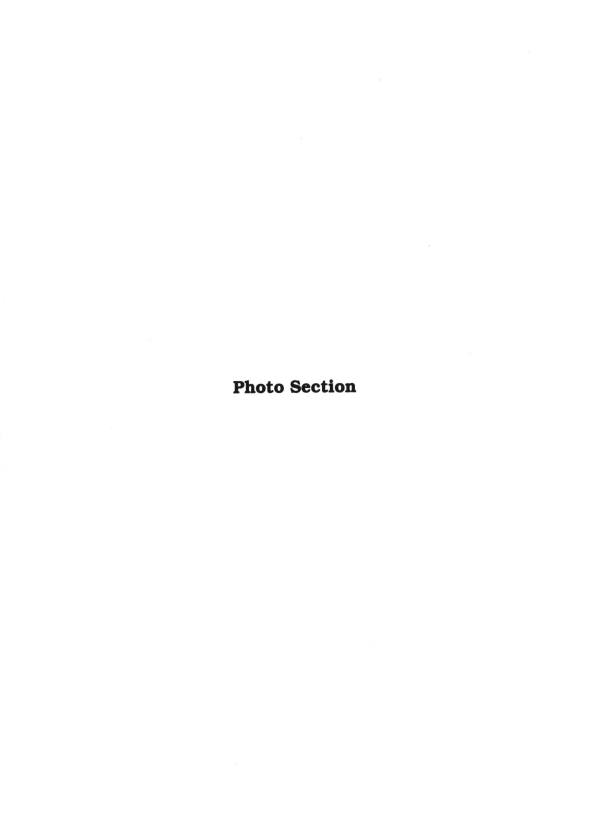

Photo Section

Army Air Corps navigation class 40-A.

One of the first formations.

Cadets in formation in front of their Quarters, the San Sebastian Hotel.

Pan American Airways hangar.

Aerial view of the Pan American Airport, Miami.

Charles Lunn greets Edgar Whitcomb upon his return from the war.

Charles Lunn and cadets aboard a navigation in-flight trainer at Dinner Key, Florida. Left to right: Lunn, Trenkle, Arnoldus, Winter, Steig, Tempest, Thomas, Whitcomb, Seamon, Dawson, and Markovich.

Charles Lunn and Norris Harbold review the wartime awards of former navigation cadets.

First instructors for US Army navigation school in World War II. Left to right front row: Eagen, Harbold, Hutchinson. Back row: Snyder, Hays, Brown, Winters, Terzian, Kiyak, Steig.

George Berkowitz reads a letter from home.

Bette and Merrill Gordon.

Theodore Boselli at bottom.

Robert Brown.

Harold McAuliff.

201

George Markovich in center.

William Meenaugh.

Walter Seamon.

202

Harry McCool.

Anthony Oliver and Francis Rang.

Harry Schreiber, Navigator of the *Swoose*.

Russell Vifquain and family.

Prelude to war, girls from the Florentine Gardens, Los Angeles. Left to right: Clark, Richards, Whitcomb, Zubko, and Sheean.

Carl Wildner and Jimmie Doolittle (Wildner at left).

Edgar Whitcomb.

Edgar Whitcomb, 22 June 1967.

Source: The Air Force Museum.

B-17D Flying Fortress, first bomber in action.

207

B-24D over a Mediterranean port.

B-25 Billy Mitchell bomber takes off from aircraft carrier *Hornet* on the Doolittle Raid.

Source: The Air Force Museum.

B-26 softening up the beach of Normandy on D day.

B-29s on a raid over Tokyo.

The *Commodore,* one of the five flying boats used in training navigators.

President Harry Truman greets Henry Myers, pilot of the first presidential airplane. Theodore Boselli on the extreme right.

Lt Comdr Lyndon Johnson in Australia.

Charles Lunn and his wife Sylvia.

Hangar 15 at Hickam Field following the 7 December 1941 attack.

212